TREATIES, LIES & PROMISES

TREATIES, LIES & PROMISES

HOW THE MÉTIS & FIRST NATIONS SHAPED CANADA

FOREWORD BY
KEVIN CHIEF

TOM BRODBECK

RONSDALE PRESS

TREATIES, LIES AND PROMISES:
HOW THE MÉTIS AND FIRST NATIONS SHAPED CANADA

RONSDALE PRESS
125A — 1030 Denman Street, Vancouver, B.C. Canada V6G 2M6
www.ronsdalepress.com

Book Design: Julie Cochrane
Cover Design: David Lester

Ronsdale Press wishes to thank the following for their support of its publishing program: the Canada Council for the Arts, the Government of Canada, the British Columbia Arts Council, and the Province of British Columbia through the British Columbia Book Publishing Tax Credit program.

Canada Council for the Arts | Conseil des arts du Canada | Canada | British Columbia Arts Council — An agency of the Province of British Columbia | British Columbia — Supported by the Province of British Columbia

Library and Archives Canada Cataloguing in Publication

Title: Treaties, lies & promises : how the Métis & First Nations shaped Canada / Tom Brodbeck; foreword by Kevin Chief.
Other titles: Treaties, lies and promises | How the Métis & First Nations shaped Canada
Names: Brodbeck, Tom, author.
Description: Includes index.
Identifiers: Canadiana (print) 20240411889 | Canadiana (ebook) 20240412923 | ISBN 9781553807162 (softcover) | ISBN 9781553807179 (EPUB)
Subjects: LCSH: Red River Resistance, Man., 1869-1870. | LCSH: Métis—Treaties—History—19th century. | LCSH: Métis—Government relations—History—19th century. | LCSH: Métis—Canada, Western—History—19th century. | CSH: First Nations—Treaties—History—19th century. | CSH: First Nations—Government relations—History—19th century. | CSH: First Nations—Canada, Western—History—19th century.
Classification: LCC E92 .B76 2024 | DDC 971.2004/97009034—dc23

At Ronsdale Press we are committed to protecting the environment. To this end we are working with Canopy and printers to phase out our use of paper produced from ancient forests. This book is one step towards that goal.

Printed in Canada

CONTENTS

. . .

Foreword

BY KEVIN CHIEF

...

ON JULY 27, 1871, at Lower Fort Garry, representatives of the Crown and Manitoba's First Nations gathered to negotiate what was to become the first of eleven numbered treaties. The day began with a colourful Anishinaabe opening ceremony and high hopes. Later that afternoon, Manitoba's lieutenant-governor, Adams Archibald, spoke of reigning Queen Victoria's aspirations: "Your Great Mother wishes the good of all races under her sway. She wishes her red children, as well as her white people, to be happy and contented. She wished them to live in comfort." It's not language we would use today—thank goodness.

I am a descendant of the "red children" of early Manitoba—Anishinaabe, from Minegoziibe Anishinabe (Pine Creek) First Nation, Treaty 4. I am also a descendant of Rosalie Chartrand, my grandmother, whose connections come from the Métis community of Duck Bay. I have only been able to officially acknowledge my Treaty 4 status since July 2021 when my claims were validated by the federal Indian Registrar's office. I had been researching and clarifying my lineage and my family stories for two years. I sourced documents and spoke to dozens of people to gather the anecdotes and evidence I needed to learn about where I come from. It was a stressful, emotional and all-consuming project.

Before that, my identity had been somewhat murky to me. My dad—Norman Chief—always said he was a "proud Indian," but he never said much else about his roots. I knew he was from Duck Bay and I knew he was a day school and residential school survivor. That was about it. He kept his sadness and trauma deep inside so my brothers and I wouldn't have to bear his pain. So there were no stories, no family trees and only a handful of photos. The trauma of his school experiences drove him to suppress much of what he knew, and it also drove him to drink to excess. The battle with alcohol ultimately took his life; he took his stories to the grave.

As a youngster and into my early twenties, without a firm grasp of my heritage, I simply identified as Aboriginal from Winnipeg's North End. I was raised near Burrows Avenue and McKenzie Street and seldom left the neighbourhood when I was young. As I grew older, I gradually began to embrace my Métis roots. It felt right—and it felt good. I was introduced to this part of my life when I was a child through my father, a singer and musician who always had a fiddler in his band. Then there were a number of special people who brought me to Métis square dances and accepted me for who I was. Today, even though I am not officially a member of the Manitoba Métis Federation, I still embrace the community's joyous spirit, jig to its rhythms and honour that part of my heritage.

Throughout my years working in community development and speaking to audiences about truth and reconciliation, I have sought to learn and understand more about the Indigenous experience in Manitoba and indeed all of Canada. In more recent years, that pursuit of knowledge became deeply personal as I worked to explore more about my identity so that my three young boys could grow to become proud Anishinaabe men.

I remain deeply committed to learning more about my Indigenous roots, for there is still much I don't know. And I know I am not alone. As the spirit of Indigenous communities across Canada is revived, and as many non-Indigenous Canadians become increasingly curious about Indigenous history in the wake of the historic Truth and Reconciliation Commission process, I believe there is an ever-increasing thirst for this knowledge.

With that as a backdrop, Tom Brodbeck's *Treaties, Lies and Promises: How the Métis and First Nations Shaped Canada* is a timely and important contribution to the discourse about the past and about the future. This well-written, meticulously researched book is a clear, straightforward telling of the events of 1869 to 1875. In these pages, you will learn how Indigenous people fought to protect their political, cultural and land rights when Canada sought to extend its jurisdiction into what is today Western Canada. You will read about how the Métis, living primarily in the Red River Settlement, and First Nations, living, hunting, and fishing across the prairies, negotiated the terms of Manitoba's entry into Canada, through the Manitoba Act and through the treaties. Manitoba is the only province in Canada whose entry into Confederation was led by Indigenous people. *Treaties, Lies and Promises* explains in great detail—and in plain language—how that came to be.

These stories are often told separately, but they all occurred in this same window of time. Learning about how these stories and communities are interrelated is critical to understanding the role Indigenous people played in establishing the terms of Manitoba's entry into Canada and how that influenced the wider settlement of western Canada. In fact, there can be no complete understanding of Manitoba's earliest days without understanding the role played by First Nations and the Métis community. The fact that Métis leader Louis Riel was (finally) officially recognized as Manitoba's first premier in December 2023 suggests that Manitobans are awakening to the truths of the province's origins.

We are living in a time of great opportunity. As Canada continues (albeit slowly) to implement the ninety-four Calls to Action of the Truth and Reconciliation Commission, we must see this as a time of optimism, creativity, communication and hard work. There have been positive strides as many Indigenous and non-Indigenous Canadians seek to break down barriers and work together to address the enduring devastation caused by the destructive and racist Indian Act, initially passed in 1876, six years after Manitoba became a province.

I believe that a path to reconciliation must be paved with goodwill, policy ingenuity and sincerity. But at the foundation of it all, we need to understand our shared history as Manitobans, Indigenous and non-Indigenous alike.

By capturing this fascinating history in such a compelling way, my friend Tom has provided Manitobans with a treasure trove of knowledge. With this knowledge, we have context. With this context, Tom has equipped us to move away from any assumptions, biases and oversimplifications that may have characterized our understanding of Manitoba's past. Instead, we can engage deeply as we try to move towards a more equitable and mutually respectful society—a society that honours the treaties, addresses the harms caused by ill-intentioned actors and creates the conditions for Indigenous communities and all Manitobans to thrive together.

Tom Brodbeck has taken it upon himself to take a deep dive into this history, to do the work necessary to tell these important stories. By taking on a task of this scope, by giving a fair and accurate account of Manitoba's earliest days, he helps strengthen the voice of Indigenous people and creates opportunities for readers to be on a journey of understanding. This book is a great gift to Manitobans and to all Canadians.

...

Kevin Chief is a member of Minegoziibe Anishinabe (Pine Creek) First Nation, Treaty 4. He is co-founder of the Winnipeg Aboriginal Sport Achievement Centre and has considerable public sector and community work experience. Kevin is a regular public speaker on Indigenous issues and plays an active role in community development in Manitoba.

Preface

. . .

WHAT STRUCK ME MOST after writing a series of feature stories in the *Winnipeg Free Press* about the Red River Resistance and the making of Canada's first treaties with First Nations was how little people knew about the history of their province and country.

Readers, including politicians, business people and others I heard from, said they had some knowledge about the armed insurrection Louis Riel and the Red River Métis waged against Canada in 1869 and 1870. However, they knew little beyond that, including the reasons behind the uprising and how it ultimately shaped Manitoba's entry into Canada.

For many, the series in the *Winnipeg Free Press* (published from 2019 to 2021 to commemorate the 150th anniversaries of Treaty 1 and the birth of Manitoba), was the first they had heard of armed Métis horsemen blocking a Canadian lieutenant-governor designate from entering their territory, or about high-powered negotiations in Ottawa between Red River delegates and senior politicians that led to the passage of the Manitoba Act.

People knew even less about the making of Treaty 1, a nation-to-nation agreement negotiated in 1871 at Lower Fort Garry between First Nations and representatives of the Crown.

It became clear to me, after the newspaper series was published, that a vacuum of information existed that needed to be filled. People wanted to know more about the history of Manitoba and Canada and the role Indigenous people played in it. I believe there is a thirst for knowledge about how those events relate to issues that confront Canada today, including the economic and social disparities that exist between Indigenous and non-Indigenous people. I began to think the time was right for a book that could further illuminate these stories.

It also occurred to me how much the events of the Red River Resistance and the making of Treaty 1 were interrelated. They took place around the same time and in the same place, with many of the same players. They were both driven by the desire of local inhabitants—mostly Indigenous—to protect their cultural, linguistic and territorial rights and to preserve their way of living. Together, they established the framework under which Indigenous and non-Indigenous people agreed to live. To fully understand the implications of that framework—and to learn more about the perceived racial superiority by white settlers and colonial governments—I believe these stories should be told together, which they are for the first time in *Treaties, Lies and Promises*.

I would like to thank the *Winnipeg Free Press* for allowing me to use the articles I wrote as the springboard and inspiration for this book. After the series ran, I delved deeper into the historical record, using primary sources, including correspondence written by government officials, Hudson's Bay Company executives and others, government annual reports, journals, legislative debates, and newspaper accounts from that period to piece together what is a riveting and dramatic period of Canadian history.

As part of Canada's renewed interest in Indigenous history, land acknowledgements have become customary across the country. The Legislative Assembly of Manitoba made history on November 29, 2021, when it opened the daily proceedings for the first time with a land acknowledgement:

> We acknowledge we are gathered on Treaty 1 Territory and that Manitoba is located on the Treaty Territories and ancestral lands of the Anishinaabeg, Anishininewuk, Dakota Oyate, Denesuline and Nehethowuk Nations.

> We acknowledge Manitoba is located on the Homeland of the Red River Métis. We acknowledge northern Manitoba includes lands that were and are the ancestral lands of the Inuit. We respect the spirit and intent of Treaties and Treaty Making and remain committed to working in partnership with First Nations, Inuit and Métis people in the spirit of truth, reconciliation and collaboration.

Yet many people still have little to no knowledge about the treaties or why reference is made to the traditional homeland of the Red River Métis. It is my hope that this book will give people a better understanding of that history and empower them to have informed discussions about Indigenous issues.

This is not an academic book. It is written deliberately to reach a general audience. Nonetheless, *Treaties, Lies and Promises* is well researched and footnoted with sources. As an experienced journalist who has spent the last thirty years researching and writing on political affairs, poring through hundreds of pages of historical documents to compile information and references for this book was a natural exercise.

But it also came after years of personal growth for me. Prior to writing for the *Winnipeg Free Press*, I was a columnist for the *Winnipeg Sun* where I wrote many columns about Indigenous issues I am not proud of. I questioned the need for a National Inquiry into Missing and Murdered Indigenous Women and Girls (MMIWG) and wrongly concluded that it was a useless exercise that wouldn't lead to change, but also that society shouldn't distinguish between race when examining homicide rates and other harms done against women and girls. I also wrote, wrongly, that it was inappropriate for courts to consider Indigenous offenders' historical background at sentencing, such as how they may have been affected by residential schools or other harmful assimilative policies (referred to as Gladue reports). When the Canadian Museum for Human Rights (CMHR) in Winnipeg announced in 2014 that it would provide free admission to Indigenous people, I criticized the policy as racist.

That was a theme that ran through many of my columns at the time: that it's never right to treat Indigenous people, or any distinct group of people within the Canadian federation, differently based on race—even through well-meaning public policy—and that it's always racist to do so. I was not only wrong and misguided, but my words caused hurt and harm to Indigenous people. They also fuelled racist sentiment among non-Indigenous people. For that, I am profoundly sorry.

There were many good reasons for the federal government to launch the MMIWG inquiry in 2015, not the least of which because Indigenous women and girls are being murdered, raped, assaulted and are going missing at disproportionate rates compared with non-Indigenous females. It is also entirely appropriate to seek ways of reducing incarceration rates of Indigenous people since they are convicted and jailed at disproportionate rates compared with non-Indigenous people, owing to the many ways Canada has mistreated and continues to mistreat Indigenous people. The CMHR's admission policy is meant to foster respect and build bridges with Indigenous communities—an important and meaningful acknowledgement I failed to recognize at the time.

I see these issues through a different lens now. I apologize from the bottom of my heart for writing those columns and am committed to finding ways of repairing the damage they caused. My hope is this book is one of many ways I can do so.

Introduction

. . .

WHEN THE HUDSON'S BAY COMPANY (HBC) reached an agreement to sell Rupert's Land to Canada in the spring of 1869, it came as a complete surprise to the people living in what is today Western Canada. They were neither consulted on the proposed annexation nor given any details about how it would affect their lives. Under the agreement, negotiated in London, England, between the British government, HBC, and Canada, Rupert's Land and the North-Western Territory[1] would be purchased by the new Dominion of Canada for £300,000 ($1.5 million in Canadian dollars at the time). HBC would retain a small portion of the land and Canada would establish a territorial government in the region, headed by a lieutenant-governor.

The inhabitants of Rupert's Land, including an estimated twelve thousand people living in the Red River Settlement—mostly French- and English-speaking Métis in what is today the core area of Winnipeg—were left entirely in the dark. There were no official visits from representatives of

---

[1] The North-Western Territory was the land northwest of Rupert's Land prior to Manitoba joining Canada. That territory, as well as land outside of Manitoba, was referred to as the North-West Territories after the province of Manitoba was created in 1870.

the Canadian government, no town hall meetings hosted by federal or British authorities, and no proclamations spelling out how existing landholdings would be treated.

From the perspective of First Nations communities living in Rupert's Land, their territory was sold without their consent. Anishinaabe, Cree and other Indigenous groups were given no information about when, or whether, treaties would be negotiated to protect their territorial and hunting rights. They learned of the proposed sale of their homeland through secondary sources. The people most affected by the largest territorial transaction in Canadian history were barely an afterthought. They played no role in the negotiations held in London and had no input into how Canada planned to assume control of the territory.

When word of the agreement reached Red River in the summer of 1869, the French Métis—led by a young and fiery Louis Riel—mobilized. They organized meetings and held emergency planning sessions throughout the settlement. Within weeks they formed an armed militia to prevent what they saw as an invasion of their homeland by a foreign entity. When a party of land surveyors from Canada arrived unannounced that summer—well before the deed of surrender with the HBC was finalized—Métis leaders drove them away.

The Rupert's Land purchase was Canada's first step towards opening the west for colonial settlement. It was scheduled to take effect on December 1, 1869. William McDougall was chosen by Canada's first prime minister, John A. Macdonald, to be the first lieutenant-governor of Rupert's Land and the adjacent North-Western Territory. The Ontario-born politician was, by Canadian standards, an ideal candidate for the job. A former federal cabinet minister and a Father of Confederation who had long advocated for Canadian annexation of the Northwest, McDougall had helped negotiate Canada's purchase of Rupert's Land from the Hudson's Bay Company in London, England, earlier that year.

McDougall travelled by train from Ottawa to Minnesota through the United States in the fall of 1869. Travelling through the United States by rail was the usual route to Red River from eastern Canada at that time. The alternative was a gruelling, weeks-long journey through the rivers, lakes and dense forests of Ontario that spanned more than one thousand kilometres. There was no railroad or telegraph directly connecting Red River to the outside world in 1869.

McDougall and an entourage of twenty people, including family members, government officials and support staff, travelled north by ox cart from St. Cloud, Minnesota, where the railroad ended in those days. The goal was to arrive in Red River before the scheduled transfer date of December 1.

The would-be lieutenant-governor had one of the finest homes in the Red River Settlement picked out for him in the parish of St. James, about ten kilometres west of Upper Fort Garry. It was said to be the most suitable dwelling in the territory for a lieutenant-governor. But McDougall would never see the inside of the St. James home, nor would he assume his position as the Queen's representative in the Red River Settlement. The lieutenant-governor designate was refused entry into the territory. He was stopped a few kilometres past the U.S. border by a party of armed French Métis, who objected to the federal government's unilateral annexation of their homeland. It was a brazen and unexpected response that escalated into a seven-month David-and-Goliath showdown between the small community of Red River and the Dominion of Canada. It would be the first chapter in the compelling story of how Manitoba became Canada's fifth province.

By the 1860s, the HBC's rule of Rupert's Land was winding down. Its delegated authority from Britain to govern the region was under increasing strain as momentum to adopt democratic institutions in the territory grew. Responsible government was already in place in eastern Canada and its expansion westward was inevitable.

Most people in Red River were not opposed to joining Canada, which had formed just two years earlier on July 1, 1867. Many Métis considered themselves British subjects and were loyal to Queen Victoria, regardless of their French, English, Catholic, Protestant or Indigenous backgrounds. Red River settlers—made up mostly of French- and English-speaking Métis[2]—celebrated Queen Victoria's birthday long before joining Canada.

What many of them objected to was joining Confederation unconditionally. They wanted input into the terms of joining Canada. When

McDougall arrived at the border, the people of Red River had no commitment from the federal government that their language, culture, landholdings or way of life would be protected. For some, blocking McDougall at the border and taking up arms was the only way to get Canada's attention.

Alexandre-Antonin Taché, bishop of St. Boniface in Red River at the time of the resistance, told a House of Commons select committee four years later that the federal government's failure to consult was the main cause of the uprising:

> When news was received that negotiations had taken place between the Canadian government and the authorities in England on the subject of the acquisition of the territory, without any attempt at consulting the population of the province, who considered themselves civilized and who were civilized, great discontent arose not only because they were not consulted, but because they were not even mentioned in the negotiations. So far as I could ascertain this discontent was universal.[3]

Robert Machray, the Anglican bishop of Rupert's Land during the resistance, came to the same conclusion. He told Canada's governor general, Sir John Young, that the conflict could have been avoided had the federal government sought local input prior to the transfer. "Persons holding official and responsible positions in this country were not consulted or even listened to . . . Had even the ordinary precaution been adopted at an early period of sending a statesman of judgement & experience like Mr. Howe[4]

---

[2] The Métis, both French and English speaking, were referred to mostly as *half-breeds* in the nineteenth century. Many Métis, including Louis Riel, used the term *half-breed*—considered less pejorative at the time than it is today—to describe themselves. This book uses the name *Métis*, who were and are the descendants of First Nations women who married European settlers and who developed a unique culture and way of life. The book distinguishes between French-speaking and English-speaking Métis where relevant.

[3] Statement by Alexandre-Antonin Taché to the Select Committee, Apr. 17, 1874, in *Report of the Select Committee on the Causes of the Difficulties in the North-West Territory in 1869–70* (Ottawa: I.B. Taylor, 1874), 9.

to test the information, that had been received, I have no doubt all would have been well."[5]

Red River, including the village of Winnipeg, was an isolated community in 1869. But it was no backwater. The region had a court system, a General Quarterly Court that met four times a year to hear criminal and civil cases, and a petty court for small claims. The settlement had schools, churches, a library, mail service, bars, hotels and farmland. A robust ox-cart trade corridor to the U.S. was developing as the buffalo hunt was winding down. An American consul was appointed to the community in the summer of 1869. Despite its isolation from the outside world, Red River was a growing and thriving community.

The District of Assiniboia, as it was also called, was rich in culture and language. It was also a relatively free community. Red River settlers were governed by the HBC through an appointed governor and a municipal-style Council of Assiniboia—made up of area residents chosen by the HBC—which administered local matters. Order was maintained largely through the consent of the people; there was little policing and no military in Red River at the time. Racial and religious tensions existed, as they did everywhere in North America. However, the Métis—both French and English, Catholic and Protestant—as well as Scottish, Irish and English settlers, First Nations and a small number of Americans and Canadians who made up the community worked, celebrated and traded together in relative harmony. When Canada came knocking, many were afraid of losing the peace they had enjoyed for decades.

The federal government's plan was to govern the region as a territory, with provincial status and an elected government to be established at a later date. Until then, it would be administered by a lieutenant-governor and a federally appointed council. Without provincial status and a democrati-

---

[4] Joseph Howe became secretary of state for the provinces on November 16, 1869, succeeding Adams Archibald.

[5] Letter from Robert Machray to Sir John Young, Mar. 18, 1870, reprinted in *Alexander Begg's Red River Journal and Other Papers Relative to the Red River Resistance of 1869–70*, edited with an introduction by W.L. Morton (Toronto: The Champlain Society, 1956), 503.

cally elected legislative assembly, there were no assurances that local inhabitants would have input into political affairs, at least not during the formative years. Red River residents were concerned that under the proposed takeover, the community would be overrun by settlers from eastern Canada, who would acquire land and disrupt the social equilibrium that had developed over generations.

Canada was warned repeatedly about the risks of assuming control of the Northwest without consulting the people who lived there. William Mactavish, the HBC's territorial governor stationed at Upper Fort Garry, was among those who advised the federal government against a unilateral takeover. He had travelled to Ottawa several months earlier and urged federal officials to consult with the people of Red River prior to annexation. His advice fell on deaf ears. Bishop Taché made the same plea. He met with federal cabinet ministers in 1869 on his way to Rome for a Vatican Council. The bishop strongly urged government to meet with local inhabitants to canvass their views and get their input on joining Confederation. "I endeavoured to cause it to be understood that serious trouble would arise, but I did not succeed,"[6] Taché told the select committee in 1874.

Alexander Begg, a Red River merchant who chronicled the events of the resistance in a detailed journal and had several letters published in eastern Canadian newspapers at the time, wrote: "It is quite apparent to intelligent people here, as it will be generally admitted in Canada when all the facts are known, that the government at Ottawa have [*sic*] made a serious mistake in the outset of their assuming the rule over the North-West."[7]

Begg's predictions proved accurate. The French Métis seized Upper Fort Garry, the HBC trading post in the heart of the Red River Settlement, on November 2, 1869. Within weeks, they declared a provisional government and demanded direct negotiations with Canada. Three months later, with the support of English-speaking Métis, the people of Red River created the region's first elected legislative assembly. John A. Macdonald, stunned by the unfolding events and taken aback by the Métis community's resolute

---

[6] *Report of the Select Committee*, Apr. 17, 1874, 9.

[7] Letter to the editor, *Toronto Globe*, Nov. 10, 1869.

defense of their homeland, agreed to negotiate with a small delegation sent from Red River. Canada's acquiescence, which culminated in the passage of the federal Manitoba Act, was a major victory for the people of Red River, one that shaped the political and cultural future of Manitoba.

First Nations, meanwhile, took no active role in the Red River Resistance. Some First Nations leaders were given assurances that treaties would be negotiated if they remained neutral during the uprising. When Manitoba's first lieutenant-governor, Adams Archibald, arrived in the new province in September 1870, First Nations Chiefs were the first to greet him at the mouth of the Red River. They demanded and secured face-to-face talks with the Crown the following year to negotiate Treaty 1.

Reaction in Canada to the resistance was largely divided along French and English lines. Many in Quebec supported the French-speaking population in Red River and their desire to protect their language and land. By contrast, much of English-speaking Ontario saw the French as treasonous and disloyal to the British Crown. The federal government viewed the uprising mostly as a misunderstanding. It claimed that the rights of the Métis and others had never been in jeopardy and that taking up arms and blocking McDougall's entry into the territory was an overreaction.

Joseph Howe, Canada's secretary of state for the provinces, defended the federal government's approach in a sternly worded letter written several months into the resistance. "At no time was the absurd idea entertained of ignoring the municipal and political rights of the people of the North-West," he wrote. "All the provinces of the British Empire which now enjoy representative institutions and responsible government have passed through a probationary period, till the growth of population and some political training, prepared them for self-government."[8] In time, the people of Rupert's Land would enjoy the same representative government as other parts of Canada, Howe wrote. He accused Métis leader Louis Riel and his supporters of mischief making and argued that they were deliberately

[8] Letter from Joseph Howe to Jean-Baptiste Thibault, Dec. 4, 1869, House of Commons sessional papers, 1870, vol. 5, no. 12, 46. Thibault was one of the two emissaries the federal government sent to Red River in December 1869.

misleading the people of Red River. Howe called their actions "rash and reckless."[9] The British Empire had a stellar record of dealing with Indigenous people, he wrote, and the same treatment would apply in the Northwest. "Everywhere within the Canadas, the progress of settlement, while it furnished new employments to the Indians, was rendered practicable by treaties and arrangements mutually satisfactory, that have formed the secure basis of the sympathy and cooperation which have distinguished the Canadians and Indians, not only since the Treaty of Paris, but from the earliest exploration of the country," he wrote. "It may fairly be assumed that the just and judicious treatment of the Indian Tribes forms the brightest page in the history of British America."[10]

Howe appeared genuinely convinced that Canada's treatment of Indigenous people was nothing short of stellar. In his final annual report as secretary of state for the provinces in 1872, he wrote that "the crowning glory of Canadian policy in all times past, and under all administrations, has been the treatment of the Indians."[11]

However, that was not the experience of Métis and First Nations people following Manitoba's entry into Confederation. Canada reneged on many of the treaty commitments it made with First Nations, some of which remain outstanding over 150 years later. Paternalistic legislation enacted in the late 1800s, including the Indian Act in 1876—designed to control the lives of First Nations and assimilate them into white culture—was neither "mutually satisfactory" nor "just and judicious." Many Métis fled Red River because they no longer felt welcome in their homeland as settlers from Canada and elsewhere poured into the region. Some were victims of violence perpetrated by white settlers, including attacks by members of the Canadian militia sent to Red River in the summer of 1870 as part of the Red River Expedition. Members of the military, headed by Colonel Garnet Wolseley, sought vengeance against the Métis, even after the provisional

---

9 Howe to Thibault, Dec. 4, 1869, 46.

10 Howe to Thibault, Dec. 4, 1869, 45.

11 Indian Affairs annual report in the year ending June 30, 1872. House of Commons sessional papers, 1873, vol. 5, no. 23, 2.

government had concluded successful negotiations with Ottawa for a peaceful entry into Canada. Commitments made to the Métis for land allotments under the Manitoba Act were bungled and took years to administer. Some Métis families received less land than promised, others were given *scrip*[12] from the federal government redeemable for land, which fell dramatically in value over time.

The Supreme Court of Canada, which issued a landmark decision on Métis rights in 2013, wrote that "the position of the Métis in the Red River Settlement deteriorated in the decades following Manitoba's entry into Confederation." Canada failed to act in accordance with "the honour of the Crown" when fulfilling its obligations under the Manitoba Act, the supreme court ruled. "White settlers soon constituted a majority in the territory and the Métis community began to unravel. Many Métis sold their promised interests in land and moved farther west. Those left amounted to a small remnant of the original community."[13]

Howe's comments were curious considering that just a few years earlier, he had been a staunch opponent of Confederation. He had waged a protracted battle against joining Canada when he was a member of the Nova Scotia legislature. Howe, who served as the Nova Scotia premier prior to Confederation, insisted Nova Scotians should decide for themselves, through a general election, whether to join Canada. Instead, it was the Nova Scotia legislature that made the decision in favour of union, without the direct consent of the people. An incensed Howe fought for months to overturn that decision, but ultimately lost. By early 1869, Howe relented and accepted a position in John A. Macdonald's federal government. A year later, as secretary of state for the provinces, Howe was lecturing the people of Red River for adopting the very position he had so staunchly taken three years earlier.

---

[12] *Scrip* was a document issued to Métis people by the federal government to comply with the land grant provision in the Manitoba Act. Scrip could be redeemed for land or its cash value.

[13] *Manitoba Métis Federation Inc. v. Canada (Attorney General)*, 2013 SCC 14, [2013] 1 S.C.R. 623.

The story of the Red River Resistance is complex. The political narrative and the events that drove the resistance, and ultimately the creation of Manitoba, were shaped by religious, linguistic and racial conflict, local infighting and a colonial mindset in Ottawa that largely disregarded the will of the people in Rupert's Land. The relationship between the Métis and First Nations was complicated. Each had their own interests but they shared a common bond in seeking the protection of their rights and way of life. Whether the armed uprising in Red River was a justified response to an overbearing colonial force or an act of disloyalty to Canada depends on who is telling the story. As the late Manitoba historian J.M. Bumsted wrote, the historical record of the resistance "can be interpreted in almost any way one chooses."[14]

The story of how Indigenous people shaped Manitoba's entry into Confederation is a compelling and riveting chapter in Canadian history. It was marked by an armed uprising, the jailing of political adversaries, a controversial execution, face-to-face negotiations with the prime minister in Ottawa and the deployment by Canada of a military expedition to Red River. Manitoba's entry into Confederation was not complete until treaties were signed with First Nations. Treaty 1 negotiations opened in spectacular fashion in July 1871 with performances by Indigenous dancers and drummers at the Stone Fort, a Hudson's Bay Company post downriver from the village of Winnipeg. About one thousand Indigenous people gathered for over a week to witness the historic talks. Chiefs representing seven First Nations bargained through interpreters during seven days of negotiations that were often heated, sometimes humorous and starkly revealing of the colonial mindset and perceived racial superiority of Crown negotiators. Treaty 2 was negotiated several weeks later, covering what is today parts of central Manitoba.

In 1875, government officials travelled throughout Lake Winnipeg by steamboat, the first vessel of its kind on Manitoba's largest lake, to negotiate Treaty 5 in what is now central and northern Manitoba. Unlike the first

---

[14] J.M. Bumsted, *Louis Riel v. Canada: The Making of a Rebel* (Winnipeg: Great Plains Publications, 2001).

two numbered treaties, Treaty 5 negotiations were held individually with multiple First Nations throughout the Lake Winnipeg area. Addendums were added to the treaty in subsequent years through follow-up talks, including with communities north of Lake Winnipeg.

The events that took place between 1869 and 1875 shaped Manitoba as we know it today and set the stage for the settlement of western Canada. They were marred by discrimination against Indigenous people, a harbinger of the federal government's assimilative policies that threatened the existence of Indigenous peoples' languages, culture and way of life. Those genocidal policies, which were concealed from First Nations negotiators during treaty talks and from Red River delegates during Manitoba Act negotiations, impacted generations of Indigenous people, the effects of which continue to be felt today. Indigenous people were assured they would be allowed to live their lives as they had prior to colonial settlement. They were misled and lied to.

CHAPTER 1

...

The Resistance

WHEN LIEUTENANT-GOVERNOR designate William McDougall and his entourage arrived at Pembina, in the Dakota Territory just south of the U.S.-Canada border, on October 30, 1869, they were shocked to find two Métis representatives waiting for them with a communiqué. The short note, written in French, ordered an indignant McDougall not to enter the territory, by order of the Métis National Committee.[1] It was signed by John Bruce, president, and Louis Riel, secretary. It was not the first act of resistance by the Métis against Canada. That summer, federal surveyors were ordered off Métis land when they arrived in the settlement months before the official transfer of Rupert's Land to Canada was scheduled to take place on December 1. In early October, Métis leader Louis Riel and others famously stood on a surveyor's chain, an act of defiance that set the stage for the coming standoff.

The HBC governor of the colony, William Mactavish, attempted without success to persuade the Métis to abandon their armed uprising. The

[1] Letter from William McDougall to secretary of state for the provinces, Oct. 31, 1869, House of Commons sessional papers, 1870, vol. 5, no. 12, 5–11.

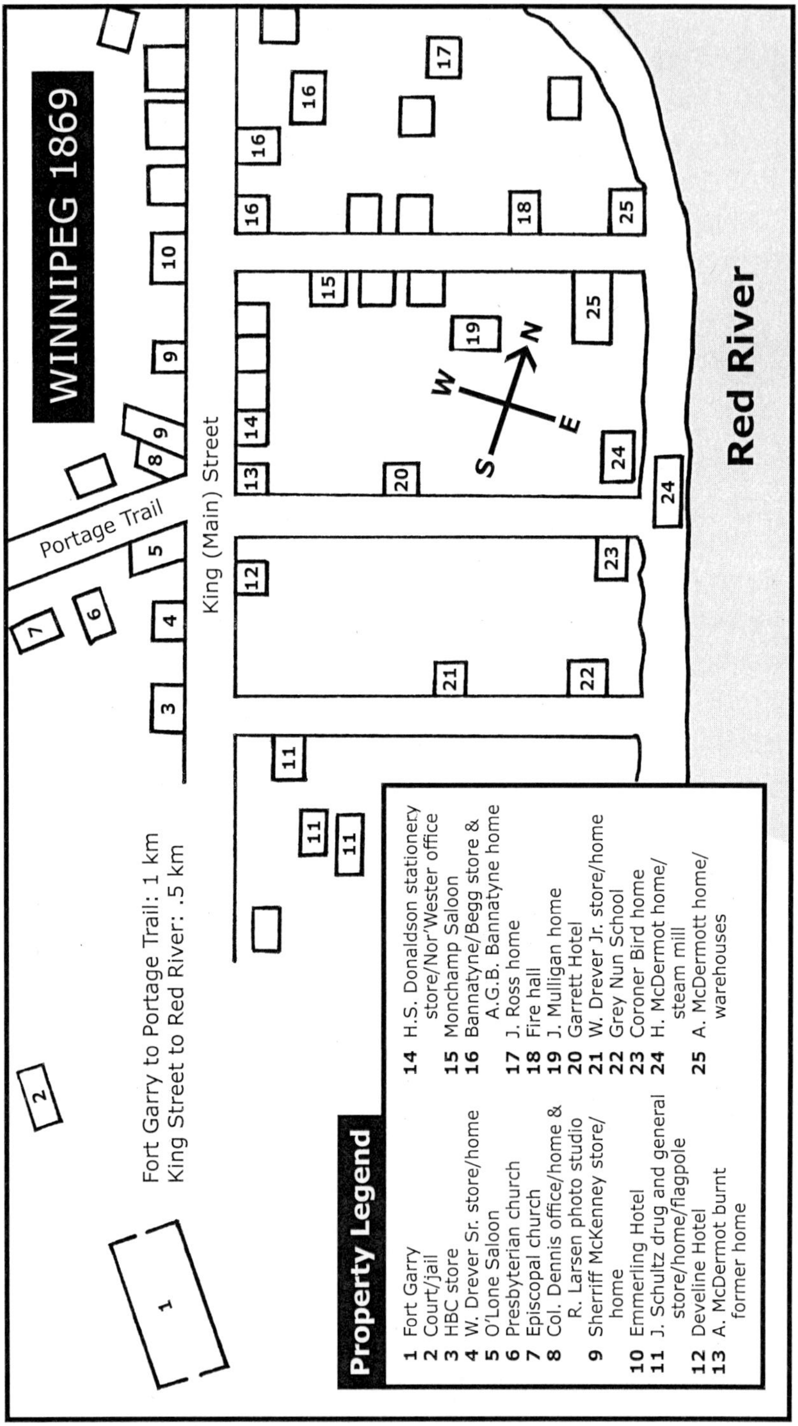

Winnipeg in 1869, when it was still a village, prior to incorporation as a city in 1873. Credit: David Malaher (2014) based on Begg (1869)

governor had some sympathy for their cause, having warned federal officials earlier that year that annexing Rupert's Land to Canada without consulting the people of Red River would trigger unrest. Nevertheless, he saw the taking up of arms as rash, unnecessary and illegal. Mactavish and the Council of Assiniboia—the official governing body in Red River at the time—called a meeting October 25 to persuade Riel and his supporters to rethink their strategy. "The council used all the arguments in their power to induce them to forgo their designs of opposing the entrance of Mr. McDougall," Mactavish wrote. "They were, however, unavailing."[2]

McDougall ignored the order not to enter the territory and moved farther north. He didn't get far. He and his group reached a small Hudson's Bay trading post a few miles north of Pembina on British soil. This time, they were confronted by a party of armed Métis horsemen who ordered them back across the U.S. border. McDougall was flabbergasted. "I asked them who sent them, and by what authority," McDougall later wrote. "They said their leaders sent them, and their authority was the government. I asked what government? They replied, 'the government we have made.'"[3]

McDougall had no military support at the time and was in no position to test the will of a group of armed Métis buffalo hunters. He returned to Pembina almost immediately. The former federal cabinet minister had been surprised by the resistance. He had heard rumours when he reached St. Paul, Minnesota, about opposition brewing in Red River over his appointment. Some Métis were unhappy with the idea that a federal politician who had negotiated the sale of their homeland without their consent was about to become their lieutenant-governor. McDougall was concerned enough about possible conflict that he left behind 350 Enfield rifles at Fort Abercrombie[4] in the care of U.S. authorities to ensure they didn't fall into the wrong hands. Still, he'd had no reason to believe he would be faced with an armed uprising that would prevent him from entering the territory. No

[2] Letter from William Mactavish to W.G. Smith, Nov. 2, 1869, House of Commons sessional papers, 1870, vol. 5, no. 12, 133.

[3] Letter from William McDougall to William Mactavish, Nov. 4, 1870, House of Commons sessional papers, 1870, vol. 5, no. 12, 30.

[4] Fort Abercrombie was an American military fort located 183 miles south of Pembina that served as a transportation hub and supply base for the area.

one had warned him about the severity of the situation, including Canada's secretary of state for the provinces, Joseph Howe, who had travelled to Red River a few weeks prior to McDougall's arrival at Pembina.

The purpose of Howe's visit to Red River in October remains somewhat of a mystery. He was in the settlement for about a week and met with several leading figures in the community, including HBC Governor Mactavish. However, he did not meet with Riel nor any of his supporters. He held no public meetings and did not consult broadly with the community to discuss the impending annexation. Howe would later claim he had paid a visit to the settlement for the sole purpose of gathering information.

James H. Ashdown, who had emigrated from Ontario to Red River a year earlier and went on to build a hardware store empire in western Canada, was one of the few prominent business people with whom Howe met. Ashdown was aware of the concerns raised by the Métis and urged the secretary of state for the provinces to meet with them to diffuse the situation. According to Ashdown, Howe refused. "Mr. Ashdown earnestly advised the famous Nova Scotian to call a public meeting and by making a clear statement of the government's intentions, disarm suspicion and meet all the objections of malcontents in open discussion," the *Manitoba Free Press* recounted some decades later. "But for some reason or other, which Mr. Ashdown says he could never fathom, Hon. Joseph Howe refused to adopt this sensible plan."[5]

Howe later confirmed during House of Commons debates on the Manitoba Act in May 1870 that he was asked to hold public meetings during his stay in Red River but said doing so could have pitted one faction of the settlement against the other and done more harm than good:

> Suppose I had called meetings and made speeches which would have had the effect of agitating the people there—one party siding with me and my views and another perhaps opposing them—what would have been said then? I would then have been told—and hon. gentlemen opposite would have been the first to say it—that the people there

[5] *Manitoba Free Press*, Sept. 11, 1919.

> were all quiet when I went amongst them, that I started them up by my speeches, that their feelings were roused and their jealousies excited by my over-anxiety for personal display—that, in fact, everything would have gone on quietly and satisfactorily if I had not set the people in motion by my maladroit statements. Sir, I was not such a fool. I am rather too old a bird to be caught in a trap like that . . . I am delighted that I resisted the invitation that was given to me.[6]

Howe crossed paths briefly with McDougall as he was travelling back to Ottawa. The encounter lasted only a few minutes and occurred during a snowstorm. His only advice to McDougall was to keep a safe distance from the small group of Canadian Loyalists[7] in the settlement to avoid agitating the French-speaking Métis. He made no mention of an armed uprising nor of trouble brewing in the settlement. That was likely because no clear signs were yet evident that an armed uprising was imminent. There is no evidence the former Nova Scotia premier was aware of Riel's plans to set up a blockade at the border to prevent McDougall from entering. Whatever was in the works by Riel and his supporters was still not widely known in the community when Howe was there, including among those with whom he met. "If there was going to be an insurrection, was it not probable that some of all these gentleman would have told me of it?" Howe said during a House of Commons debate. "Was it likely that there could be such a thing known to these honourable gentlemen, and yet none of them impart it to me? Surely not a man of them knew of it, and if not a man of them knew of it, how was I to find out?"[8]

Despite that statement, McDougall would later accuse Howe of failing to warn him about the hostilities brewing in the settlement. During acrimonious debates in the House of Commons the following year, McDougall

---

6 House of Commons debates, 1st Parliament, 3rd Session, vol. 1, May 9, 1870, 1469–70.

7 Canadian Loyalists in Red River were English-speaking settlers mostly from Ontario whose outspoken and unconditional support for joining Canada was not always well received by the Métis.

8 House of Commons debates, May 9, 1870, 1470.

even claimed, without evidence, that Howe had aided and abetted the "rebels" while he was in Red River. Howe denied the allegation.

After he was escorted back over the U.S. border, McDougall had little choice but to remain in Pembina. He could not immediately communicate with Ottawa and was uncertain about what to do next, except to await further instructions from federal officials. He was entirely unprepared for the events that unfolded around him. In a letter to Howe on November 5, he wrote:

> Our position is beset with difficulties. We cannot go forward without an armed force, which is not at our command. We cannot immediately return for our horses require rest and grain before we can undertake so long a journey. The snow may overtake us on the way, and rendered further progress with wagons impossible. There are no houses or supplies between this place and Georgetown, a distance of 150 miles. With the Canadians who joined me on the way, and who are now afraid to go forward, my party numbers twenty souls.[9]

McDougall had no sympathy for the Métis and their cause. He saw them as rebels and "malcontents" who were engaged in an illegal takeover of HBC territory. As far as he was concerned, the insurgents were disloyal to the Crown and ought to be defeated. The lieutenant-governor designate was able to gather some intelligence from the settlement. He had allies in Red River who opposed the resistance and who served as his informants. Through them he communicated frequently with HBC governor William Mactavish and others to seek ways of toppling the Métis, although he would find no strong ally in Mactavish. The governor wanted peace but not at the cost of violence.

The idea of sending a delegation to Pembina to escort McDougall into the territory was raised among some who opposed the resistance, but it was short-lived. Some feared that doing so would result in a violent clash with

---

9 Letter from William McDougall to secretary of state for the provinces, Nov. 5, 1869, House of Commons sessional papers, 1870, vol. 5, no. 12, 21.

the French Métis. By then, several hundred armed men loyal to the Métis cause were prepared to fight. Any attempt to overthrow them would have likely resulted in bloodshed.

Mactavish continued to attempt to persuade the Métis to lay down their arms, but his words fell on deaf ears. There was no use. Once it was clear Riel and his supporters would accept nothing less than full bilateral talks with Canada, Mactavish wrote to McDougall and urged him—for his own safety and to maintain the public peace—not to enter the settlement. "It is to be feared that your coming into the settlement at the present moment would not be free from considerable danger," he wrote.[10]

McDougall concurred. However, he wasn't prepared to give up just yet. With allies in the settlement, McDougall believed he could organize a counterinsurgency capable of defeating the Métis. He had no mandate from Ottawa to do so, nor was it a realistic option. Nevertheless, he planned to stay put to see if he could assemble a force strong enough to push his way into the settlement. "We all agreed that it would be discouraging to our friends, and a great triumph for the rebels, if their first demonstration resulted in my return to Canada before I had assumed the reins of government. We therefore resolved to remain at Pembina for a week or two longer, if we could get supplies."[11]

The Métis continued to secure the territory. They erected a barricade[12] across the roadway at St. Norbert south of Upper Fort Garry and deployed armed, mounted guards to police the trail between Red River and the U.S. border. Anyone coming into the territory was checked for credentials and queried about the nature of their business. It was the closest thing to martial law the small community could muster.

On November 2, the same day McDougall was forced back to Pembina, a party of Métis seized Upper Fort Garry. The Métis needed a base for their operations and the HBC fort, which acted as both a trading post and the

---

10 Letter from William Mactavish to William McDougall, Oct. 30, 1869, House of Commons sessional papers, 1870, vol. 5, no. 12, 24.

11 McDougall to secretary of state for the provinces, Nov. 5, 1869, 21.

12 La Barrière Park in the rural municipality of Ritchot is named after this historic event.

seat of government in the colony, was the ideal facility. The move was also a clear demonstration that Riel and his men were assuming control of the settlement.

It was a remarkably easy and bloodless coup. A group of armed Métis walked through the unsecured gates and announced they were taking possession of the fort. There was no resistance from HBC officials and little they could do to prevent the takeover. The fort—a compound made up of several buildings surrounded by a stone wall—was not protected by armed guards and the District of Assiniboia had no military. A Royal Canadian Rifles detachment had been stationed in Red River from 1857 to 1861. After its departure, the settlement operated with little policing. Only a handful of constables protected the community, and they were no match for several hundred Métis buffalo hunters.

Mactavish described the takeover this way:

> A number of these daring people, suddenly, and without the least intimidation of their intention to make such a move, took possession of the Gates of Fort Garry, where they placed themselves inside and outside the Gates, to the number in all of about one hundred and twenty, and where, night and day, they have constantly kept a pretty strong armed guard.
>
> On being asked what they meant by such a movement upon the fort, they said their object was to protect it. Protect it from what? They were asked. Their answer was—from danger. Against what danger, they were asked? To this question, they replied that they could not now specify the danger, but that they would do so hereafter, and obstinately took up the position they have since kept in spite of all our protests and remonstrances, at such a bold and high-handed proceeding.[13]

Seizing Upper Fort Garry was strategically important for several reasons. The fort contained months' worth of food and supplies, firearms,

---

[13] Letter from William Mactavish to William McDougall, Nov. 9, 1869, House of Commons sessional papers, 1870, vol. 5, no. 12, 53–54.

ammunition, financial records, and cash—enough to get the Métis through the winter. No one knew how long the resistance would last, nor how it would end. The fort housed the HBC governor and his staff and contained important records such as land titles and tax records.

For Riel and his supporters, having possession of Fort Garry was also important to guard against outside forces. Not everyone in Red River supported the armed uprising. The majority either opposed it, at least during the early stages of the resistance, or had no direct involvement in it. The staunchest opponents were a small group of Canadian Loyalists who abhorred the idea of French Catholic Métis interfering in the annexation process. They would become the chief opponents of the resistance and the greatest threat to the French Métis. Many were arrested and jailed in makeshift prisons at Upper Fort Garry during the uprising.

The federal government was alarmed at the events unfolding in Red River. John A. Macdonald and his cabinet were caught off guard. They were deeply concerned about where the resistance could lead, including how it might reverberate in eastern Canada. "The crisis was grave as it was unexpected, and might, if dealt with rashly and unwisely, lead to a civil if not a national war, the end of which no man could foresee," Howe wrote to McDougall in late November.[14]

The federal government misunderstood the purpose of the uprising. Joseph Howe initially interpreted it as an act of disloyalty to the British Crown. "The insurrection you describe is not merely an expression of dislike to the Government of the Dominion, but an open violation of Imperial legislation and defiance to the authority of the Crown," he wrote to McDougall.[15] The Métis, however, were not challenging the authority of the British Crown, nor were they rejecting Canada per se. Many of them, including Riel, expressed loyalty to the British Crown throughout the resistance.

In late October, prior to the takeover of Upper Fort Garry, an elected national committee of French-speaking Métis was established. It was the

---

[14] Letter from Joseph Howe to William McDougall, Nov. 29, 1869, House of Commons sessional papers, 1870, no. 12, 32.

[15] Howe to McDougall, Nov. 29, 1869, 33.

first incarnation of a Métis governing body. Riel was elected secretary and John Bruce, a St. Norbert carpenter, was president, although in name only. Riel emerged as the true leader of the movement. He had broad support among the French Métis, who made up about half the population of Red River in the fall of 1869. But he also had his detractors, including some from within the francophone community. The English-speaking settlers, including the anglophone Métis, were particularly skeptical of Riel's methods. Most opposed the armed uprising and expressed their misgivings about it. They were adamant that blocking McDougall at the border was a grave error.

Riel was only twenty-five years old at the time, but highly educated and bilingual after studying for the priesthood in Montreal as a teen (though he never became a priest). Like his father Louis Riel Sr.—who decades earlier had fought for Métis trading rights in Red River—Riel had natural leadership skills and a keen sense of the political environment around him. Even though the French-speaking Métis slightly outnumbered the English, Riel knew that presenting a united front to Canada was an important factor in establishing legitimacy. He needed their support.

Four days after taking the fort, Riel issued a public notice inviting one representative from each of the ten English-speaking parishes in the area, and two from Winnipeg, "to consider the present political state of this country, and to adopt such measures as may be deemed best for the future welfare of the same."[16] Despite their opposition to the armed uprising, the English speakers agreed to meet, if for no other reason but to keep the peace. They sent a representative from each parish. It was a small but important victory for the French Métis.

The meetings were tense. They took place under heavy guard in the small courthouse outside the walls of Fort Garry between November 16 and December 1. An estimated 150 armed French Métis protected the building. The meetings, which were closed to the public, got off to a rocky start. The delegates were welcomed with a twenty-four-gun salute, a gesture the English-speaking representatives objected to. They saw the use of firearms

[16] Public notice issued Nov. 6, 1869, by Louis Riel, House of Commons sessional papers, 1870, vol. 5, no. 12, 39.

to begin a meeting as hostile and inappropriate. "The English express their dissatisfaction with these joyous demonstrations of gunfire," Riel wrote in his notes of the meetings. "They protest to a man against this display of military force. The French are more light-hearted and explain to them that they have no hostile intention toward their English compatriots."[17]

Henry Prince, Chief of the St. Peter's band (Peguis First Nation) and the only First Nations member at the meetings, also expressed unease with the brandishing of firearms. He said that among his people "it was customary to attend council without arms when peaceably inclined."[18] The Anishinaabe Chief, accompanied by a bodyguard, also lamented during the second day of meetings that he had not been allowed to express his opinions during the first day of proceedings. He was on the verge of boycotting the rest of the meetings, he said, but ultimately decided to attend.

Prince's presence at the November meetings was one of the rare instances of First Nations involvement in the Red River Resistance. For the most part, First Nations did not participate in the movement. It is unknown what Prince contributed to the November sessions, if anything. Riel makes no mention of him in his notes. Furthermore, Prince was there as an English-speaking delegate, not as a First Nations representative. No designated First Nations representatives were invited to the meetings.

Riel opened the proceedings by urging the delegates to take immediate steps to protect their rights as inhabitants of Red River: "My dear fellow citizens, because of our attachment to British institutions which we respect as you do, let us not wait together until our liberties pass to alien power. Let us not wait to claim them, until they may be in other's hands."[19]

The Métis leader's opening address did little to ease opposition among the English, who continued to express disapproval of the armed uprising and the decision to block McDougall at the border. They agreed Red River

---

[17] Riel's handwritten notes of the meetings have been preserved and are part of the Riel Papers, reprinted in *Alexander Begg's Red River Journal and Other Papers Relative to the Red River Resistance of 1869–70,* edited by W.L. Morton (Toronto: The Champlain Society, 1956). Entry from Nov. 16, 1869, 420.

[18] Riel Papers, *Alexander Begg's Red River Journal*, entry from Nov. 17, 1869, 172.

[19] Riel Papers, *Alexander Begg's Red River Journal*, entry from November 16, 1869, 421.

settlers should have input into the terms of joining Canada, but rejected the methods used by the French. Riel explained that if McDougall were allowed into the settlement, even under the guise of negotiating the terms of entry into Confederation, they would lose the leverage they had. Once McDougall was sworn in as lieutenant-governor, Riel argued, there was no guarantee he would be willing to negotiate. Keeping him at bay gave the people of Red River an upper hand. Besides, McDougall had no authority to negotiate on behalf of the federal government. He had been appointed solely with a mandate to install a non-elected, territorial government in the Northwest.

The most spirited exchanges at the meetings took place between Riel and James Ross, the unofficial leader of the English Métis. Ross, a one-time part owner of the local *Nor'Wester* newspaper, was one of twelve English representatives at the meeting. Like Riel, Ross was born in Red River, was relatively young at age thirty-four and was also educated in eastern Canada. He was articulate, well-informed and could easily match Riel's sharp wit and nimble debating skills. The two leaders sparred frequently throughout the resistance but were also political allies at times.

Ross and many of the other English delegates disapproved of the decision to seize Fort Garry, seeing it as an act of disloyalty to the Crown. When Ross demanded to know why the French had seized the fort, Riel said it was "to preserve it for the inhabitants of the country," and to ensure McDougall could not use it to rule the settlement "as absolute master." Besides, it was customary for the Métis to take up arms against any threat to the community, Riel explained, including against "Indian war parties." Blocking McDougall at the border was no different. "Having been repelled, he is still there just over the line, wearing us down, trying to establish himself here as our master, declaring himself already our master without our authorities having told us that he is,"[20] said Riel. Ross countered that seizing the fort and undermining the authority of the Hudson's Bay Company was "unconstitutional." He said that Mactavish, as HBC governor, was still the representative of the Queen. He accused the French of occupying the fort "in spite of him." Talks became heated.

[20] Riel Papers, *Alexander Begg's Red River Journal*, 421.

Governor Mactavish, who was still stationed at Upper Fort Garry, drafted a proclamation demanding the insurgents return the fort to HBC control. He submitted it to the delegates, who agreed to read it aloud at the next meeting. Ross immediately seized on Mactavish's demands, citing the proclamation as official word from a representative of the Crown that the French were guilty of sedition. Ross insisted that Riel and his supporters immediately relinquish control of the fort. "I hope that they are going to do it for their own benefit and the satisfaction of their relatives and friends, the English of the colony," Ross said.[21] Riel refused. Under no circumstances would the French give up the fort, he said, prompting another fiery exchange between the two Métis leaders. "Your acts are now acts of rebellion," Ross charged. Riel countered that holding the fort was not rebellion against the British Crown. "If we rebel against the company which sold us and against Canada which wishes to buy us, we do not rebel against the English government, which has not yet given its approval to the actual transfer of the country . . . we wish that the people of Red River be a free people. Let us help one another."[22]

The delegates met again the next day. The English speakers continued to argue that McDougall should be allowed into the settlement to negotiate. If, during negotiations, he refused to guarantee the people of Red River their rights, he could again be expelled, they suggested. Riel would have none of it, saying that if McDougall were brought into the settlement and sworn in as the Queen's representative, any attempts to banish him would be construed as a rebellion against the Crown. There was a difference between blocking a lieutenant-governor designate at the border and overthrowing a Queen's representative once installed in office. Riel understood that important distinction. It was the main reason he took a hard stance against allowing McDougall into the settlement. After further debate, deliberations adjourned until November 22 to allow the General Quarterly Court to resume sitting in the courthouse.

Both sides agreed that joining Canada would benefit the Red River Settlement and the surrounding area. However, they remained at loggerheads

---

21 Riel Papers, *Alexander Begg's Red River Journal*, 422.

22 Riel Papers, *Alexander Begg's Red River Journal*, 422.

over the process of getting there. Riel was adamant that direct negotiations with federal officials in Ottawa should be pursued, while the English-speaking delegates continued to favour a dialogue with McDougall. Neither side would budge.

The gap widened further when deliberations resumed and Riel raised the spectre of declaring a provisional government, a proposition that shocked even some of his own supporters. The Métis leader said creating a temporary government was necessary to protect the community and to create a governing body that could negotiate with Canada to "force it to grant us a form of responsible government."[23] Ross was aghast. He warned that Canada could send troops to quash the resistance if the settlement established its own government. Not likely, Riel countered. With no accessible winter route to the west, and the near impossibility of U.S. officials allowing Canadian or British troops to travel by train through its territory, the settlement had until the spring to secure a deal with Canada. Declaring a provisional government would help, not hinder, that process, said Riel. "We have six months before us," he said confidently. "During that time, we shall have a settlement with Canada."[24] His prognostication proved accurate.

Convincing the delegates to establish a provisional government would be one of Riel's greatest challenges, even among the French Métis. Several influential members of the Métis community, including Charles Nolin, François Dauphinais and Baptiste Tourond, were not easily persuaded. Riel met with the French delegates separately overnight in a marathon session on November 23 that lasted seven hours. According to Riel, some of the French Métis were afraid to declare a provisional government because they thought it could be seen as a rebellion against the Queen. "What fears and hesitations there were to overcome," he wrote.

The Métis leader eventually won over the French delegates. He convinced them that establishing a provisional government, with or without the English, was necessary to protect their rights and way of living. Gaining

---

[23] Riel Papers, *Alexander Begg's Red River Journal*, 425.

[24] Riel Papers, *Alexander Begg's Red River Journal*, 426.

the support of influential members of the French Métis community was a significant victory for Riel and a key part of establishing the solidarity required to negotiate with Canada, even if the English delegates were not immediately on board.

Riel proposed the idea of a provisional government to the full assembly at the November 24 meeting. He suggested the governing body would include an equal number of French and English representatives to ensure the settlement was fully represented. He made an impassioned plea that this was the most effective way to negotiate with Canada. But the English delegates were still not convinced. Most neither rejected nor embraced the idea of a provisional government and wanted more time to assess their options. They said they would have to consult their constituents before agreeing to such a drastic move. The meeting was adjourned until December 1.

In the meantime, the French Métis began drafting what would be the first of many versions of a "list of rights," conditions Canada would have to meet to establish authority in Rupert's Land. It included the protection of language, religious, democratic and land rights, as well as a requirement that Ottawa negotiate treaties with First Nations "to ensure peace on the frontier."[25] The list would evolve over the following five months, but it formed the basis of what a Red River delegation would take to Ottawa in the spring of 1870 to negotiate Manitoba's entry into Canada.

The list of rights was shared with the English delegates. Much like the prospect of a provisional government, they neither opposed nor endorsed the list, at least not immediately. For the most part, they were reluctant to support what the French were proposing because they weren't convinced their own land and democratic rights were in serious jeopardy. The English-speaking delegates, mostly Protestants, did not have the same concerns as their French Catholic counterparts, many of whom feared they would be overrun by English-speaking Protestants from Ontario. "The English section of the community is not less anxious about their rights and about the prosperity of the country than the French," the settlement's Anglican

[25] "List of rights" approved Dec. 1, 1869, House of Commons sessional papers, 1870, vol. 5, no. 12, 100.

bishop, Robert Machray, wrote a few months later. "But they have never entertained a doubt that in due time everything that would be advantageous for the country would be granted by Canada."[26] It explains, at least partially, why the English-speaking Métis were less emboldened than their French-speaking counterparts to take drastic action to protect their rights.

The anglophone delegates returned to their parishes for more consultation. After several days, they returned with a decision: they would not take part in the formation of a provisional government. They considered the move reckless and counterproductive. The French Métis would have to go it alone, a setback that didn't appear to discourage Riel. "Go," Riel told the English representatives, "return peacefully to your farms. Rest in the arms of your wives. Give that example to your children. But watch us act. We are going to work and obtain the guarantee of our rights and of yours. You will come to share them in the end."[27]

Creating a provisional government was no easy task. One problem was the timing; exactly when to make the declaration was tricky. The Hudson's Bay Company had title to the land until December 1. Overriding the company's authority before then, through a formal declaration of self-government, might be seen in eastern Canada as an illegal takeover. However, once the HBC's title expired and there was no lieutenant-governor present to assume control, Riel and his French Métis believed they would have the legal authority to establish their own government. As long as McDougall was stuck in Pembina and unable to exercise authority, a provisional government could fill the legal void.

It appeared John A. Macdonald was aware of that reality. The prime minister's first move, after learning that McDougall was prevented from entering the settlement, was to delay transfer of the territory to Canada. He instructed Canada's governor general, John Young, to cable Britain on November 26 to request a postponement of the transfer date. Canadian

---

[26] Letter from Robert Machray to Governor General John Young, Mar. 18, 1870, *Alexander Begg's Red River Journal*, 505.

[27] Riel Papers, *Alexander Begg's Red River Journal*, 428. Riel's handwritten notes of the sessions.

officials complained to the British government that they could not accept the transfer "unless quiet possession can be given."[28] They refused to ratify the sale of the territory while it was under the control of insurgents.

Macdonald's protest marked the beginning of a prolonged rift between Canada, the HBC and the British government over whose responsibility it was to ensure a peaceful transition of the territory. The HBC said it bore no responsibility to maintain political stability in the settlement at the time of transfer. As far as the company was concerned, it was buyer beware.

Ironically, there had been peace in the land until Canada deployed land surveyors to Red River prematurely and appointed McDougall as lieutenant-governor without consulting the people who lived there. Despite that, Macdonald blamed the HBC, claiming the company should have warned Canada about trouble brewing in the settlement prior to the transfer. "If they were aware of the feeling of discontent, they ought frankly to have stated it to the imperial and Canadian governments," he wrote. "If they were ignorant of the discontent, the responsibility of such willful blindness on the part of their officers must rest upon them."[29] William Mactavish, the HBC governor at Fort Garry, rejected Macdonald's interpretation of events. He said he had in fact warned the federal government earlier that year during a trip to Ottawa that Canada should consult with the people of Red River prior to the transfer to avoid a backlash. Canadian officials later denied that Mactavish ever offered such words of caution. Rupert's Land was quickly turning into a political hot potato between Britain, the HBC and the federal government.

Britain balked at Canada's assertion that it was the HBC's responsibility to hand over the territory in a state of peace. With no military in the Red River Settlement and very little policing, the company had no ability to quash the uprising even if it wanted to, the imperial government stated. "Throughout these negotiations it has never been hinted that the company

---

28 Letter from Governor General John Young to Lord Granville, Nov. 26, 1869, House of Commons sessional papers, 1870, vol. 5, no. 12, 142.

29 John A. Macdonald, copy of a report by a committee of the privy council, Dec. 16, 1869, House of Commons sessional papers, 1870, vol. 5, no. 12, 142.

is to be bound to hand over its territory in a state of tranquility," Lord Granville, Britain's secretary of state for the colonies, wrote. "Rather, its inability to secure that tranquility, and the dangers resulting from that inability to the neighbouring Colony, is taken for granted as a reason why its responsibilities should be adopted by Canada."[30] Government officials in London agreed to postpone the transfer but were not happy about it.

Macdonald believed that as long as the HBC had title to Rupert's Land, any formal declaration of a provisional government by the Métis would have no legitimacy. However, because Ottawa had no immediate communication with McDougall, the lieutenant-governor designate was not aware that Ottawa had postponed the transfer date. The right hand did not know what the left hand was doing. Earlier, McDougall had been instructed not to declare Canadian authority in Red River until he received authorization from Ottawa. "As matters stand, you can claim or assert no authority in the Hudson's Bay Territory, until the Queen's proclamation, annexing the country to Canada, reaches you through this office," Howe reminded McDougall in a November 19 letter. "It will probably be issued on the 2nd December, and will be forwarded by a safe hand as soon as received."[31]

It was clear McDougall was to do nothing until he got word from Ottawa. However, the lieutenant-governor designate was growing impatient. He had been stuck at Pembina with his family and staff in makeshift quarters for a month and was irate that he was still barred from entering the settlement. He wrote to the secretary of state for the provinces in November saying that if he didn't get official word soon on the date of the transfer he would be "embarrassed," and the insurgents would be emboldened. "They understand perfectly that I have no legal authority to act, or to command obedience, till the Queen's proclamation is issued."[32]

---

30 Letter from Lord Granville to Governor General John Young, Nov. 30, 1869, House of Commons sessional papers, 1870, vol. 5, no. 12, 142.

31 Letter from Joseph Howe to William McDougall, Nov. 19, 1869, House of Commons sessional papers, 1870, vol. 5, no. 12, 14.

32 Letter from William McDougall to secretary of state for the provinces, Nov. 13, 1869, House of Commons sessional papers, 1870, vol. 5, no. 12, 39.

In the same letter, he condemned Mactavish for failing to maintain authority at Fort Garry. He even suggested the HBC governor might have aided and abetted the Métis. "I cannot account for this extraordinary reticence and hasty surrender of authority by the legal rulers of the country upon any theory but that of the weakness and imbecility of the Governor, and the complicity of some members of his council with the insurrection."[33] The allegation that Mactavish and his officials might have assisted the Métis in their insurrection, including intentionally allowing them to take possession of Upper Fort Garry, was raised repeatedly in Ottawa. It was always denied by Mactavish. The allegation was investigated by the HBC the following year, but no evidence was ever found to support the claim.

McDougall, no longer willing to wait for official word from Ottawa, decided to take matters into his own hands. On December 1 he issued his own proclamation, in the name of the Queen, that Rupert's Land was now in the hands of Canada. The move was both reckless and illegal, a grave error that would later enrage federal officials. He crossed the border in the middle of the night with several members of his party and read the proclamation to a dark, empty plain. He also had the proclamation printed and distributed in the settlement by his Canadian supporters in Red River. Although the proclamation was illegal, the people of Red River could not have known it at the time. Like McDougall, they had not yet received word from Ottawa that the transfer of Rupert's Land to Canada had been delayed. As far as they were concerned, McDougall's proclamation had been sanctioned by the Crown. It gave the appearance that HBC rule had been extinguished, which in turn gave the Métis, at least in their minds, the right to declare a provisional government.

McDougall didn't stop there. He took steps, without authorization from Ottawa, to create a militia to overthrow Riel and his supporters. He appointed John Stoughton Dennis—one of the surveyors sent by the federal government the previous summer—as "lieutenant and conservator of the peace." Dennis's mission, which was published and distributed throughout the settlement, was to "raise, organize, arm, equip and provision, a sufficient

[33] McDougall to secretary of state for the provnces, Nov. 13. 1869, 37.

force" to "attack, arrest, disarm, or disperse the said armed men [Riel and the Métis] so unlawfully assembled and disturbing the public peace."[34]

It was, for all intents and purposes, a declaration of war against the Métis. Riel and his supporters could not have known McDougall was acting on his own. As far as they knew, this was an attempt by the federal government to topple the resistance by force. Riel called it a "commission to make war on us."[35] The move emboldened the Métis and hastened their plans to declare a provisional government. McDougall's call to arms occurred around the same time the French and English delegates were meeting in late November.

If Riel and the Métis needed any further justification to declare a provisional government, this was it. They did so officially on December 8, issuing the "Declaration of the People of Rupert's Land and the North-West." It outlined how Rupert's Land had been sold by the Hudson's Bay Company to Canada earlier that year, "by transactions with which the people were considered unworthy to be made acquainted."[36] It stated that under the law of nations, people had a right to establish their own government when "the power to which it was subject abandons it, or attempts to subjugate it, without its consent to a foreign power." It went on to state that "we refuse to recognize the authority of Canada, which pretends to have a right to coerce us, and impose upon us a despotic form of government still more contrary to our rights and interests as British subjects, than was that Government to which we had subjected ourselves, through necessity, up to a recent date." The declaration also stated that the provisional government was prepared to begin talks with Ottawa, further evidence that the Métis were not opposed to joining Canada. Two days later, a provisional govern-

---

[34] Commission appointing J.S. Dennis as lieutenant and conservator of the peace, Nov. 1869, House of Commons sessional papers, 1870, vol. 5, no. 12, 105.

[35] "Memoir by Louis Riel on the Course and Purpose of the Red River Resistance, Written in 1874," in *Alexander Begg's Red River Journal and Other Papers Relative to the Red River Resistance of 1869–70*, edited by W.L. Morton, 532. Toronto: The Champlain Commission, 1956.

[36] "Declaration of the People of Rupert's Land and the North-West," issued Dec. 8, 1869, House of Commons sessional papers, 1870, vol. 5, no. 12, 99–100.

ment flag was hoisted at Upper Fort Garry and the Métis celebrated with gunfire salutes, drink and music from the St. Boniface Boys' Brass Band. A sense of victory and empowerment spread across the settlement.

John A. Macdonald had been outmanoeuvred. The prime minister and his cabinet were furious, mostly at McDougall for overstepping his legal authority by issuing a bogus proclamation and attempting to assemble a militia at Lower Fort Garry (the HBC post downriver from the Red River Settlement, also known as the Stone Fort). Meanwhile, Dennis recruited a few hundred Indigenous and non-Indigenous locals to join the militia and began running drills at the fort. He documented which parishes the recruits were drawn from. However, after several days of preparation and military exercises, the campaign was abandoned. The troops were never deployed. Dennis had been convinced by locals that any attempt to use force to overthrow the provisional government could lead to a bloody civil war. "Pray do nothing aggressively," James Ross wrote to Dennis on December 6. "A civil war is altogether too dear a price to pay for anything wanted on either side. Many others think so too."[37] No blood had been spilled until then and most settlers wanted to keep it that way; so did the federal government. "Any hasty attempt by the Canadian government to force their rule upon the insurgents would probably result in armed resistance and bloodshed," wrote Macdonald. "Every other course should be tried before resort is had to force."[38]

Meanwhile, in a scathing letter from Howe, McDougall was severely reprimanded for overstepping his authority:

> As it would appear from these documents that you have used the Queen's name without her authority—attributed to Her Majesty acts which she has not yet performed—and organized an armed force within the Territory of the Hudson's Bay Company, without warrant or instructions, I am commanded to assure you that the grave occurrences which you report have occasioned here great anxiety . . . the

---

[37] Letter from James Ross to J.S Dennis, Dec. 6, 1869, House of Commons sessional papers, 1870, vol. 5, no. 12, 120.

[38] Macdonald, Dec. 16, 1869, 143.

> proceedings of Colonel Dennis, as reported by himself, are so reckless and extraordinary, that there can be no relief from solicitude here while an officer so imprudent is acting under your authority.[39]

McDougall would not see that correspondence until after he returned to Canada. It took a week or longer to deliver mail between Ottawa and Pembina. After the failed attempt to organize a militia, and with the provisional government at Fort Garry showing no signs of backing down, the lieutenant-governor designate had few cards left to play. By mid-December, still unable to enter the territory and growing frustrated with the sparse living conditions at Pembina (and unlikely willing to endure a prairie winter), McDougall began planning his return to Ottawa. In one last act of desperation, he wrote Riel directly. After hearing that the Métis leader was expected to travel to a Hudson's Bay Company post near the U.S. border, he pleaded for a face-to-face meeting:

> Sir, – I hear from the Hudson Bay Post that you are expected to arrive there from Fort Garry tonight. I send this note to inform you that I am anxious to have a conversation with you, before answering despatches which I have recently received from the Dominion Government.
>
> I have not yet had any communication from you or anyone else, on behalf of the French half-breeds who have prevented me from proceeding to Fort Garry, stating their complaints or wishes in reference to the New Government. As the representative of the Sovereign to whom you and they owe, and as I am told, do not wish to deny allegiance, it is proper that some such communication should reach me. It will be a great misfortune to us all, I think, if I am obliged to return to Canada, and hand over the powers of Government here to a military ruler.
>
> This will be the inevitable result unless we find some solution of the present difficulty very soon. I have full powers from the Govern-

---

[39] Letter from Joseph Howe to William McDougall, Dec. 24, 1869, House of Commons sessional papers, 1870, vol. 5, no. 12, 83–85.

> ment, as well as the strongest desire personally to meet all just claims of every class and section of the people. Why should you not come to me and discuss the matter? I beg you to believe that what occurred will not affect my mind against you or those for whom you may be authorized to speak. The interview proposed must be without the knowledge or privity of certain American citizens here who pretend to be en rapport with you. I trust to your honour on this point.[40]

Riel did not respond to the invitation; there is no evidence he received the correspondence. Even if he had, his lack of response would have been of little surprise, given McDougall's threat that the "inevitable result" of Riel's failure to open a dialogue with him would be the installation of a "military ruler."

By this time, the events at Red River were attracting attention in the United States. Americans had developed a robust trading network with the settlement and a small number of U.S. citizens were living there. Naturally, they had an interest in the region, particularly once news broke of an armed insurrection and the seizing of a major HBC post. The possibility of a U.S. takeover of the Northwest, or some parts of it, was always on the minds of Canadian officials. However, it was not a significant or imminent threat at the time. For the most part, Americans were simply curious about what was transpiring in the north. It wasn't long before the resistance drew extensive coverage in U.S. newspapers. The *St. Cloud Journal* reported on the early stages of the resistance in late November, under the headline "Progress of the revolution at Red River":

> Operations thus far have been carried on mainly by the French half-breeds, the English half-breeds and whites having taken no part, though being in full accord with the movement. At present only six hundred men are under arms, but it is reported that in the spring the number will be increased to three thousand.[41]

---

40 Letter from William McDougall to Louis Riel, Dec. 13, 1869, House of Commons sessional papers, 1870, vol. 5, no. 12, 95.

41 The number of armed Métis never grew that large. It reached approximately 800 armed insurgents at the peak of the resistance.

> On the second of November, Fort Garry and the government house were taken possession of by the insurgents in the name of the Provisional Government which they have organized. The St. Paul Press has advices which say that the capture was accomplished by a piece of quiet strategy. During the morning about sixty half-breeds, armed with their usual flint-locks, strolled into the inclosure in small parties, until at a preconcerted signal, while the officers and servants—there being no troops—were at dinner, they took possession of different buildings and commanded a surrender, which was quietly yielded, resistance being useless. No violence was offered the officials, and they were left undisturbed. . . .
>
> Martial law has been proclaimed and the very best order prevails. The American residents have remained non-committal, but they are ready to aid the insurgents should necessity require. Gov. McDougall and party are at Pembina, on American soil, where they will probably remain during the winter. The Governor is endeavoring, by negotiations, to settle the difficulty without a resort to arms. It is said that the Red River people are not making this movement to throw off their allegiance to the Queen, but to oppose annexation to Canada.[42]
>
> Unless our Government should commit the great folly of permitting the Canadian government to send troops through Minnesota and Dakota, any attempt made by the Dominion to coerce the people of Red River cannot but prove futile. Even with that permission, years of war and thousands of soldiers would be required to bring the insurgents to any kind of terms. They have the cordial sympathy of the people of the North-West, if not of the whole country.[43]

As late as November 29, McDougall was still under the illusion he could organize a military coup to overthrow the provisional government, take

---

[42] The American *St. Cloud Journal* would later learn that Red River residents were not opposed to annexation with Canada. Rather, they wanted to negotiate the terms of entry into Confederation.

[43] *St. Cloud Journal*, Nov. 25, 1869.

Riel prisoner and gain control of Upper Fort Garry. "If the measures I have taken to organize an armed force to seize Riel and his colleagues, and disperse the rank and file of his followers, should prove successful, the provisions will soon be again in our possession," he wrote.[44]

By mid-December, it was obvious McDougall's efforts were futile; he had few reasons left to remain in Pembina. His continued presence and his attempts to thwart the actions of the provisional government only strengthened Riel's resolve. Mactavish urged McDougall to return to Canada "for the peace of the country."[45]

Surprisingly, the federal government still wanted McDougall to remain at Pembina, even after learning of his unlawful proclamation and his unauthorized attempt to organize a militia. Howe instructed the lieutenant-governor designate to stay put until it was safe to enter the settlement. "We hope that calmer counsels will soon prevail, and that these misguided people will disperse. So soon as they do, you will, I presume, proceed to Fort Garry and carry out your instructions."[46]

But McDougall left Pembina before he received that correspondence. He and his entourage packed up and departed for St. Paul, Minnesota, on December 18. They were back in Canada by January. It was a humiliating experience for the former cabinet minister and one that would alter the rest of his political career. He later resumed his position in Parliament as an MP, but he fell out of favour with Macdonald and his cabinet.

---

[44] Letter from William McDougall to William Mactavish, Nov. 29, 1869, House of Commons sessional papers, 1870, vol. 5, no. 12, 65.

[45] Mactavish to McDougall, Nov. 9, 1869, 54.

[46] Letter from Joseph Howe to William McDougall, Dec. 7, 1869, House of Commons sessional papers, 1870, vol. 5, no. 12, 42.

CHAPTER 2

...

The Convention of Forty

AS 1869 WOUND DOWN, the French Métis were still struggling to persuade the settlement's English-speaking population to join the resistance. By the end of December, most anglophones in Red River still neither actively opposed nor supported the new provisional government. Only a small group of Canadian Loyalists—some of whom were still trying to find ways to bring McDougall into the territory as late as mid-December—were openly hostile towards Riel and his supporters. The majority of anglophones, including the English-speaking Métis, remained largely neutral for the time being.

Riel knew that establishing a governing structure, even without the support of the English, would be an important step towards negotiating a settlement with Ottawa. The new year would bring more unrest, new challenges and a controversial decision by Riel and the provisional government that would forever change the complexion of the resistance. In the meantime, those who joined the cause were now in a stronger position to negotiate the terms of entry into Confederation. The Métis had an organized structure in place to respond to whatever Canada had to offer.

For John A. Macdonald, the resistance was both a surprise and a thorny political problem he knew he could not solve overnight. His first attempt to defuse the uprising was to send two emissaries to Red River in December—Charles de Salaberry and Jean-Baptiste Thibault. Both men failed to make any progress in changing the minds of the Métis, largely because neither was given the authority, nor the mandate, to negotiate with Red River residents. Sending troops to Red River to quash the resistance was out of the question. The only way to access the territory in the winter was by train through the United States to St. Cloud, Minnesota, and by sled to Red River. American authorities would have blocked any attempt by Canada and England to send troops through their territory. Besides, no one wanted bloodshed, Maçdonald and the British government included.

The prime minister's next move was to send a special commissioner to Red River with a broader mandate and a more convincing sales pitch. He chose Donald A. Smith, a Hudson's Bay Company executive stationed in Montreal, for that mission. Smith left Ottawa on December 13. He travelled by rail to St. Cloud and by wheeled carriage to Abercrombie, where he procured a sleigh for the remainder of the journey. Smith met with McDougall on his way past the U.S. border. "From him I learned how serious the aspect of affairs had latterly become at Red River," Smith would later write.[1] When Smith arrived at Fort Garry, he was immediately questioned by Riel, who inquired about the purpose of his visit. The HBC executive, who stayed at the fort and was not permitted to leave the premises, was aghast at what he found. "The state of matters at this time, in and around Fort Garry, was most unsatisfactory, and truly humiliating," he wrote. "Upwards of sixty British subjects were held in close confinement as 'political prisoners;' security for persons or property, there was none."[2]

Smith's mission was to win over the settlers, defuse the armed resistance and, if possible, bring the settlement into the Canadian fold. It was a tall order. Smith was not on friendly terms with Riel, who he saw as an agitator

---

1 Report from D.A. Smith to Joseph Howe, Apr. 12, 1870, vol. 5, no. 12, 1. Smith issued a full report to Parliament upon his return to Ottawa, which was submitted as this sessional paper.

2 Smith to Howe, Apr. 12, 1870, 1.

and whose influence he attempted to undermine. He refused to acknowledge the legitimacy of the Métis provisional government (he referred to it as a "so-called provisional government") and sought to mobilize support against Riel. He later boasted that he had "detached many of the leading men among the French from Riel."[3]

Some saw Smith's real purpose in Red River as more deceitful—that the true intention of his mission was to undermine Riel's leadership by using bribes to divide and conquer the settlement. His terms of reference from Ottawa stated that the federal government would honour "any pecuniary arrangements that you may make with individuals, in the manner we spoke about." It was unclear exactly what that meant. It may have been a green light to offer cash, or promises of employment, to anyone willing to lay down their arms and abandon Riel's provisional government. Louis Schmidt, a Riel confidant who served in the provisional government, would later allege that Smith used the promise of money to try to lure supporters away from Riel. "He attempted to detach as many *métis* as possible from the popular cause and he used for that purpose the means which succeed so often with weak spirits, even when they are not mercenary: money, which he did not lack."[4]

There is, however, no other evidence that Smith bribed anyone in Red River. But by mid-January he did succeed in weakening the resolve of some Riel supporters, at least temporarily. That changed after Smith persuaded Riel to hold a public meeting—which would ultimately backfire for Smith—to allow the commissioner to communicate directly with the people of Red River. For Smith, a public meeting was an opportunity to address the fears many had in the settlement that by joining Canada they might lose their democratic, linguistic and land rights. For Riel, it was a

3 "The Ottawa Diary of Sir Stafford Northcote," in *Manitoba: The Birth of a Province*, vol. I, ed. W.L. Morton (Altona: Manitoba Record Society Publications, 1965). Northcote, governor of the Hudson's Bay Company, was in Ottawa during negotiations between Red River delegates and federal officials and recorded his observations, including meetings he had with many high-ranking officials, among them Donald A. Smith.

4 "Memoirs of Louis Schmidt," written in 1912 and reprinted in *Alexander Begg's Red River Journal and Other Papers Relative to the Red River Resistance of 1869–70*, edited by W.L. Morton (Toronto: The Champlain Commission, 1956), 469.

chance to shore up support and reinforce his message that entering Confederation should only occur after face-to-face negotiations with the federal government.

The public meetings, held over two days, were a turning point in the resistance. They were held outdoors in frigid temperatures in the courtyard of Upper Fort Garry and drew hundreds from around the settlement. They included lengthy speeches from Smith, Riel and others and ultimately led to the political union of the French and English Métis, as well as the creation of the settlement's first elected legislative assembly.

About one thousand people bundled up on the bone-chilling afternoon of January 19, 1870, and made their way by foot or sled to Fort Garry. It was a large gathering for a community of twelve thousand people, and no building in the settlement was large enough to hold it indoors. On the first day, people huddled together for five hours in −20 degrees Fahrenheit (−29°C) weather to hear the words of Donald A. Smith. Red River–born Métis Thomas Bunn chaired the meeting. Judge John Black, head of the General Quarterly Court, was secretary. Riel, leader of the fledgling and still fragile Métis provisional government, served as interpreter for the French-speaking attendees. It was "the most important meeting ever held in the settlement,"[5] Bunn told the crowd as they opened the proceedings.

Smith wasn't authorized to negotiate with the settlers. Still, his mandate was more substantive than those of the first two delegates Macdonald had sent. He began by reading aloud several letters from Ottawa, including details of his commission and assurances to the people of Red River that their rights would be protected when Rupert's Land joined Canada. Some of the letters had been written in the early weeks of the resistance, including one from Lord Granville, Britain's colonial secretary, to Canada's governor general, John Young, dated November 26, 1869. It was a sternly worded yet hopeful message from Queen Victoria:

> The Queen has heard with surprise and regret that certain misguided persons have banded together to oppose by force the entry of the

---

[5] *Alexander Begg's Red River Journal*, entry from Jan. 19, 1870, 265.

> future Lieut-Governor into our territory in Red River. Her Majesty does not distrust the loyalty of her subjects in that settlement; and can only ascribe to misunderstanding or misrepresentation, their opposition to a change planned for their advantage. She relies on your government to use every effort to explain whatever misunderstandings may have arisen, to ascertain their wants, and conciliate the good will of the people of Red River Settlement. But in the meantime, she authorizes you to signify to them the sorrow and displeasure with which she views the unreasonable and lawless proceedings which have taken place; and her expectation that if any parties have desires to express or complaints to make respecting their condition and prospects, they will address themselves to the Governor-General of Canada. The Queen expects from her representative that as he will be always ready to receive well founded grievances—so will he exercise all the power and authority she entrusted to him, in the support of order and the suppression of unlawful disturbances.[6]

The crowd cheered, apparently happy to hear a message from the Queen. The response was not surprising—the majority of Red River settlers were loyal to the British Crown, including Riel and his supporters.

Most of the first day was taken up by Smith reading aloud several lengthy letters and other correspondence. The meeting was adjourned to the following day when, despite the frigid weather, an even larger crowd turned out. Community interest was growing. Indigenous clergy Reverend Henry Cochrane was added to the stage to translate the proceedings into Cree. Smith opened the proceedings with a long and impassioned appeal to the crowd, insisting that joining Canada would be in their best interest and would improve their standard of living. He also assured them that their democratic and property rights would be protected and that Ottawa would be prepared to negotiate further details with representatives of the community. The people of Red River would have the same rights as other Canadians, said Smith. It was an enticing proposition.

---

[6] *New Nation,* Jan. 21, 1870.

Smith's presence in the settlement was the first time a representative from Canada had spoken officially and directly to the people of Red River on the prospect of joining Confederation. Until then, no one from Ottawa had given them the time of day. As cold and uncomfortable as it was standing for the better part of an afternoon in the Fort Garry courtyard, those in attendance were interested in what the special commissioner had to say. The HBC executive was an eloquent and convincing speaker; he piqued the interest of the crowd and appealed to their sense of attachment to the land. He spoke of having blood relatives in Rupert's Land and feeling a deep attachment to the people in the territory. He even vowed to resign his position with the Hudson's Bay Company if he thought it would lead to the peaceful union of Rupert's Land with Canada—a pledge that was likely more political theatre than a genuine willingness to sever ties with the company to which he had dedicated his professional career. "Hence though I am myself a Scotchman, people generally will not be surprised that I should feel a deep interest in this great country and its inhabitants," said Smith, prompting cheers from the crowd. "I am here today in the interests of Canada, but only in so far as they are in accordance with the interests of this country."[7]

The federal government was now prepared to take a more conciliatory approach with the people of Red River. For the most part, it was forced to. Faced with an armed resistance and the creation of a provisional government, Ottawa had little choice but to open a dialogue with them. Talk was cheap, however. Smith had no authority to conclude a formal agreement. While he made some headway in convincing the crowd that joining Canada would be in their best interest, he did not have a mandate to negotiate the finer points of an agreement. There were still many outstanding issues, including what form of government would be installed in the settlement. Ottawa wanted to annex Rupert's Land as a territory, governed by a federally appointed lieutenant-governor and council. Macdonald promised provincial status with an elected legislative assembly, but only once the territory was more established.

There were risks inherent in that plan for Red River settlers. Delaying

[7] *New Nation*, Jan. 21, 1870.

representative government would allow Canadians from the east to emigrate to the new territory in large numbers, decreasing the odds of Métis residents winning seats in a future provincial legislature. Riel was aware of that dynamic. It was one of the reasons he was adamant that Manitoba enter Canada with full provincial status and an elected legislative assembly, a position not everyone in Red River agreed with at the time.

Riel was up next to speak. It was a defining moment for the Métis leader, who had struggled in the weeks leading up to the mass meeting to maintain solidarity among his supporters. Smith's speech had been convincing; Canada would ensure that the rights of local inhabitants would be protected and they would have a say in how their lives were governed, the crowd was told. Still, there was no proposed act of Parliament to guarantee those rights, only well-meaning but nonbinding correspondence from Ottawa. Many questions around land and other rights still had to be negotiated. Those could only be resolved through direct talks with authorized officials in Ottawa.

Riel, though young and relatively inexperienced, was a naturally gifted and persuasive speaker. His formal education in Montreal and his short stint as a law clerk there had provided him with valuable insight into the machinery of government and the intricacies of Confederation. Smith may have presented an effective sales pitch on the broad benefits of joining Canada, but Riel delivered a strong rebuttal. He reminded the shivering crowd that negotiating an agreement in writing to protect their property, democratic rights and linguistic rights was a critical piece of the puzzle. The Métis leader closed with an impassioned speech:

"I came here with fears—we are not yet enemies," Riel told the crowd, drawing loud cheers. "But we came very near being so. As soon as we understood each other, we joined in demanding what our English fellow subjects in common with us believe to be our just rights . . . I am not afraid to say our rights; for we all have rights. We claim no half rights, mind you, but all the rights we are entitled to. Those rights will be set forth by our representatives, and, what is more, gentlemen, we will get them."[8]

Riel struck a chord with the crowd. With his ardent words, the Métis

[8] *New Nation*, Jan. 21, 1870.

leader persuaded French and English settlers to establish an elected body to negotiate directly with Canada. Riel moved a motion to create a convention of forty delegates—twenty French and twenty English—to consider Smith's commission and develop an action plan to begin talks with the federal government. The motion passed. For the first time during the resistance, the French and English Métis would join forces to create a political union that would carry them into Confederation.

Riel found himself once again at the forefront of the movement. He regained most of the support he had lost since Smith's arrival. The armed resistance, while controversial and opposed by many, had succeeded in getting the federal government to the negotiating table. It had done so, at least until that point, without bloodshed. Four months after William McDougall was prevented from entering the settlement, the prime minister of Canada was now prepared to engage in face-to-face negotiations with delegates from Red River. Several weeks after the January meetings, the prime minister put that commitment in writing: "In case a delegation is appointed to proceed to Ottawa, you can assure them that they will be kindly received, and their suggestions fully considered," Macdonald wrote. "Their expenses coming here and returning, and whilst staying in Ottawa, will be defrayed by us."[9] For the small community of Red River, it was a remarkable achievement.

Elections to select delegates for the Convention of Forty were held immediately following the public meetings. Representatives were chosen from each of the French and English parishes. Unlike at the Métis National Committee's November sessions, English-speaking delegates were now full participants. They agreed to draft a list of rights that would be taken to Ottawa.

Convention of Forty deliberations began on January 26. The opening sessions, held in the courthouse outside the walls of Upper Fort Garry, were productive. Proceedings were held in French and English, with Riel and

---

[9] Letter from John A. Macdonald to Bishop Taché, Feb. 16, 1870, submitted to House of Commons select committee, 1874, in *Report of the Select Committee on the Causes of the Difficulties in the North-West Territory 1869–70* (Ottawa: I.B. Taylor, 1874), 19.

James Ross chosen as translators. Judge John Black was selected as chairman. Several articles were drafted and approved with little contention during the first week of talks, including a plan to send three delegates to Ottawa to negotiate with federal officials. Riel was later nominated as one of those delegates but declined, saying his responsibility was to remain in Red River to govern the settlement.

It wasn't until the convention tackled the thorny issue of provincial status that the sessions turned acrimonious. Debate over whether Manitoba should enter Confederation as a province or a territory sparked conflict, not only between French and English Métis delegates, but also among some French Métis representatives. Riel introduced a motion for provincial status during a subcommittee of council, but it was defeated. The majority of the Convention of Forty supported the federal government's position that Rupert's Land, including Red River, should enter Canada as a territory, with provincial status to come later, but Riel disagreed. Unwilling to concede defeat, he raised the issue again at full council, ten days into the deliberations.

Riel had the support of only seventeen of the forty members—a minority. Three of the francophone Métis elected to the convention, including Charles Nolin, one of Riel's chief political adversaries, opposed him on several issues. The other twenty delegates represented English-speaking parishes. On contentious motions such as provincial status, Riel could not count on the support of all twenty French delegates. He was overruled on more than one occasion.

The Métis leader argued that provincial status was necessary to ensure that the settlement had a representative government to control its own affairs, including when it came to landholdings. He sought the same legislative powers as Canada's four existing provinces. Riel was well versed in the legal division of powers between the federal and provincial governments under the British North America Act of 1867, Canada's constitution. As a territory, he said, Red River would not have the same local powers as provinces in the east, including an elected legislative assembly, during the crucial period of early settlement. "As to this question of a province, let me ask, is it not possible for us to settle our own affairs in a satisfactory manner? Cannot we make regulations for outsiders, with reference to the sale and disposition of our lands? This land question, and that of our means of raising money, constitute perhaps the principal points in the whole provincial arrangement."[10]

His opponents, including James Ross, disagreed. For now, the English delegates were satisfied with entering Canada as a territory; they said the settlement wasn't prepared to take on full provincial status. Once the Northwest expanded its population, gained political experience and grew its tax base, it could then graduate to provincehood. "Our position, if we entered as a province, would be very different than that of the other provinces," Ross said. "They entered the Dominion entirely equipped with roads, bridges, court houses, etc. They entered as full-grown men and having everything. We are here asking to be admitted as men, when, in respect to our equipment and outfit, the country is only in its infancy." Ross questioned whether the settlement, if it was granted immediate provincial status, would have the resources and tax base to pay for the infrastructure and public services it would need to grow and trade with the rest of Canada. As a territory, under the direct governance of Ottawa, the federal government would be obliged to fund those services and capital costs. Besides, Ross added, Ottawa would never agree to allow the settlement to enter as a province. The sparring between Ross and Riel carried over from the national committee meetings in November. "It is the first time you have had no ambition," Riel quipped.

Judge John Black, later chosen as one of the delegates sent to Ottawa to negotiate with the federal government, was also opposed to seeking immediate provincial status. Like Ross, he argued that the settlement was not

---

[10] The proceedings of the Convention of Forty meetings were recorded by William Coldwell, an experienced newspaper reporter with strong shorthand skills. He was a co-founder of the *Nor'Wester*, the first newspaper in Red River. His reporting of the convention's meetings was published in the local *New Nation* newspaper. Donald A. Smith, who was present at the meetings, described the *New Nation*'s reporting of the proceedings as "sufficiently exact" in his report to Parliament. All quoted material on these pages concerning the Convention of Forty meetings, unless otherwise indicated, is from the *New Nation* newspaper, Feb. 4, 11, 18, 1870 editions.

ready for provincehood and that Ottawa would not grant it in any case. "Those provinces which have been already admitted into Confederation, have been long accustomed to exercise the honors of self-government," said Black. "They have population, wealth, importance, and dignity, which do not belong to us in this infancy of our days. What then is the use of our spending time in the discussion of a matter which is practically hopeless?" Black, who remained as recorder of the settlement's General Quarterly Court[11] during the resistance, warned that the offer to enter Confederation as a territory could be jeopardized if they demanded too much. "We have now within our reach something valuable," he said. "But if you hanker too long about it—if you dilly-dally too long—it may be that this opportunity will pass away. I do therefore most earnestly say to you, gentlemen, waste no time needlessly, take the tide as it now is, at the full, take it and I believe you are safe and will be prosperous."

Black also argued that just because Canada and the United States might be interested in acquiring the Northwest, the people of Red River should not make the mistake of overstating its value. He used a colourful metaphor, evoking laughter among the delegates: "May we not, in this respect, be running the risk of making the same mistake the beautiful flirt sometimes does, who with a long train of ardent admirers, dallies and coquettes first with one, then with that, and then with the other—not knowing which of the adoring swains to choose, until at last she finds herself obliged to put up with a very hum-drum sort of mortal after all?" As a community, the Red River Settlement might have been "dazzled" by all the attention, but it didn't have the population or the resources to take on provincial status. "While we want this dignity," Black said, "we do not see how we ourselves are able to bear the expense of reaching it. We therefore propose that the Confederation of Canada should erect, as it were, all the scaffolding by which we are to be carried up to this point of dazzling grandeur."

Riel replied to Black's lengthy speech: "I think the chairman's speech is admirable—its words are very fine—but it has not the power to convince."

---

[11] The term *recorder* was the name used for judge in the District of Assiniboia in the nineteenth century. Black was the fourth and last recorder of the General Quarterly Court.

But much to Riel's chagrin, Black's speech and influence was persuasive enough that the delegates rejected the idea of immediate provincehood. A motion to end discussion on the matter, and to join Canada as a territory, was moved by John Sutherland of Kildonan. It was seconded by Alfred Boyd, an English-speaking merchant living in the parish of St. John's who would later become Manitoba's first provincial secretary. "It seems to me most important that we should first enter the Dominion as a territory, and in due time take our position there as a province," said Boyd. Riel said in French (interpreted by Ross[12]) that Sutherland's motion to end debate was "simply an exhibition of fear" and accused him of being a coward. Riel saw no reason why they should not attempt to attain the higher status of becoming a province to govern their own affairs. "I, too, am an English subject, but I do not wish to be so to excess," Riel said. "I never heard a more unreasonable request than that now made, and in attempting to choke off discussion in a matter of so much importance, Mr. Sutherland has shown himself not to be the man for us. I move an amendment that the discussion be continued." Sutherland countered that he was simply there to represent the people who voted him onto council. "I have the good of the country at heart," he said. "And if I had not, I would not have been going round these last few months without fee or reward." Riel relented, saying he had not meant to attack Sutherland personally. "I spoke of Mr. Sutherland as the representative of a certain district—not personally. Personally I have a high respect for him, believing him to be a good representative and an honest man." The heated debates, which descended into shouting matches at times, underscored the conflict that still existed between the many factions in Red River, not only between English- and French-speaking delegates, but also among the French.

Riel's motion to continue discussion on the matter was carried 20 to 19. But that vote was short-lived. After further debate, council voted 24 to 15 in favour of joining Canada as a territory. Riel had lost. The vote was a setback for the Métis leader, but it would not be the final word on provincial status.

---

[12] Ross and Riel, while often political foes during debate, translated for each other when Riel spoke in French and when Ross spoke in English.

Riel moved on to other matters. The following day, he introduced a motion to nullify the Hudson's Bay Company's sale of Rupert's Land to Canada. Riel wanted that included in the list of rights delegates would take to Ottawa. Under the terms of the sale, HBC was entitled to receive up to one-twentieth of the territory's fertile land, east of the Rockies, south of the Saskatchewan River and north of the American border. Riel objected to that provision, as did many First Nations. Indigenous leaders argued that the HBC had no right to sell the land in the first place and by doing so subverted the interests of the Métis and First Nations. The sale of Rupert's Land should be renegotiated between Ottawa and the people of Red River, without HBC involvement, Riel insisted.

The English delegates disagreed. Riel, feeling betrayed, grew more frustrated. "The truth of it is, the half-breeds of the country must govern, with the other portion of the people if they are together," he said. "For four months the English-speaking population stood aloof and took no part in the movement. But now they come forward and try to cut down the rights to half rights." Riel warned of dire consequences if the English and the French failed to unite in a common cause. "We have braved Indians and white men in maintaining our present position. And if we do not all join in support of the present order of things there will probably be massacre—not perhaps immediately, but within two years."

Riel's appeal failed. The motion to renegotiate the sale of Rupert's Land was defeated 22 to 17. The English delegates and a handful of French Métis voted against it. Riel was furious. He marched up and down council chambers and accused the three French members of the convention who voted against him of being traitors. "The vote may go as it likes; but the measure which has now been defeated must be carried," Riel said. "It is a shame to have lost it; and it was a greater shame because it was lost by those traitors." He pointed to several council members, including Nolin, who jumped to his feet and said in French, "I was not sent here, Mr. Riel, to vote at your dictation. I came here to vote according to my conscience. While there are some things for which we blame the company [HBC], there is a good deal for which we must thank them. I do not exculpate the company altogether, but I say that in time of need we have often been indebted to them for assistance and kindness."

Riel countered that he had "friends" who were determined to add the defeated motion to the list of rights. It is unclear what he meant by that or which "friends" he was referring to. However, it was an example of how Riel, when opposed, was not above circumventing the will of an elected body. He eventually abandoned the HBC land sale issue. The proposal was never pursued by the delegates in Ottawa. However, Riel's demand that the settlement enter Canada with provincial status did make it onto the list of rights that went to Ottawa, despite the convention's opposition to it. It was too important an issue for Riel to drop.

The mood at the meeting worsened. Riel turned to the French section of the convention and accused them of undermining the efforts of those fighting for the rights of Red River settlers. "Your influence as public men is finished in this country," said Riel, speaking rapidly and pointing threateningly at Nolin and others. Nolin again challenged Riel: "Let me tell Mr. Riel that I was sent here by my parish. I never sought the position and personally, if I am lost to public affairs, I would be rather glad of it. You, Mr. Riel, did what you could to prevent my coming here and failed; and if it suited my purpose to come back again, I would come at the call of my parish, in spite of you." Alexander Begg, who attended most of the Convention of Forty proceedings, recorded in his journal that "Riel said the convention had beaten him this time, but he would beat them yet."[13] Begg also reported a month later that Riel jailed Nolin at Fort Garry "on account of his having accused Riel during the late convention of having tried to interfere with his (Nolin's) election as a delegate."[14]

The Convention of Forty wrapped up after two weeks of debate. Despite the heated exchanges, the convention managed to find consensus in a number of areas. A new list of rights was approved and three delegates would be sent to Ottawa to negotiate with the federal government. The list of rights differed somewhat from the one the French Métis had drafted in December. But it had similar items in it: the protection of land rights; bilingualism in the courts and the legislative assembly; the right to an elected council; demands for a railroad to connect Red River to the east; and several clauses

[13] *Alexander Begg's Red River Journal*, entry from Feb. 5, 1870, 296.

[14] *Alexander Begg's Red River Journal*, entry from Mar. 7, 1870, 331.

about taxation and how land would be organized. Like the December list, it included a demand that treaties be negotiated with First Nations. After the convention was adjourned, a copy of the list of rights was given to Donald A. Smith for his review and consideration. He had no authority to accept or reject the demands. However, he did say most of them would likely be accepted by federal officials.

Riel was still very much in charge of the settlement at the time. He continued to hold prisoners at the fort even after promising that all prisoners would be released following the election of the Convention of Forty delegates. While there were some democratic principles that had driven the formation of the national committee and the Convention of Forty, Riel still called the shots. When his authority was challenged, he ruled with an iron fist, sometimes with threats of violence and death. Yet he commanded hundreds of armed and skilled Métis buffalo hunters who remained loyal to his cause throughout the resistance. No group or faction within the settlement could match that. Those who tried, failed, and often found themselves behind bars.

Still, Riel's preference was to seek unity among the French, English and others in the settlement, which he ultimately succeeded in doing. He was keenly aware that presenting a common front to Canada would strengthen the bargaining position of the delegates in Ottawa. Nevertheless, Riel's message was clear: if others did not want to join the French Métis in demanding the rights of Red River settlers, he and his supporters would do so on their own. If anyone got in their way, blood would spill.

Meanwhile, for the most part, First Nations continued to remain neutral during the resistance. Much like at the national committee meetings in November, they played only a small role in the Convention of Forty debates. Reverend Henry Cochrane, who provided translation services in Cree during the January meetings at Upper Fort Garry, served as the St. Peter's band delegate. However, like Henry Prince, who had represented the band during the November sittings, Cochrane was officially recognized as an English delegate, not a First Nations one. No delegate positions were reserved specifically for First Nations representatives. There is some evidence that promises were made to them that if they remained neutral during the resistance, treaties would be negotiated to protect their lands and way of life. It is unclear who made those commitments, but it may partly explain why they did not take a more active role.[15] Still, their patience began to wear thin as the resistance dragged on. According to Alexander Begg, tension was brewing between some First Nations and the Métis: "The Indians in and around the Indian Settlement are very much discontented and declare that if the French are not out of Fort Garry by the spring, they will attack them. Hy [Henry] Prince, the chief, is very bitter on the subject and told Bishop Taché during his Lordship's late visit that if an Indian stole an axe or an old blanket he was severely punished but that the French had been plundering wholesale all winter."[16]

Riel recognized the need for First Nations to pursue formal agreements with the Crown. The requirement that Ottawa negotiate treaties with First Nations was included in every version of the list of rights during the resistance. "The Indians have visited us in great numbers, they are hungry as grasshoppers," Riel wrote to Bishop Taché that summer. "The treaties engage their attention. What prudence must be employed when dealing with these people!"[17] However, for reasons that were never clear, demands that the Crown negotiate treaties with First Nations did not make it to the negotiating table in Ottawa during talks between Red River delegates and federal officials. Manitoba's First Nations would have to wait over a year to negotiate their first treaty, which occurred at Lower Fort Garry in the summer of 1871 with Treaty 1.

Several versions of the list of rights were drafted during the Red River Resistance. The one produced by the Convention of Forty would not be the final one delegates would take to Ottawa. It was amended in the weeks leading up to the departure of the delegation, although it is unclear by whom. Some amendments may have been made unilaterally by Riel, in-

---

[15] Manitoba's first lieutenant-governor, Adams Archibald, refers in correspondence with Ottawa to previous commitments made with First Nations Chiefs to negotiate treaties. Chapter 8 provides greater detail.

[16] *Alexander Begg's Red River Journal*, entry from Mar. 29, 1870, 347.

[17] Letter from Louis Riel to Bishop Taché, July 24, 1870, in *Report of the Select Committee*, 37.

cluding the demand that Manitoba enter Canada with provincial status. As promised, Riel would not allow the matter to die. Granting Manitoba immediate provincial status (and by connection an elected legislative assembly) would give local Métis the chance to run for public office and secure seats in the legislature. Riel warned as early as October 1869 at a Council of Assiniboia meeting that if Red River joined Canada without the protection of its democratic rights, the Métis could be crowded out of their homeland. It was a constant theme in Riel's speeches. He elaborated on it during the Convention of Forty debates when the matter of voter eligibility was being discussed. "We must not by our own act allow ourselves to be swamped," said Riel. "I do not wish in anything I may do to hurt the stranger, but we must, primarily, do what is right and proper for our own interests. In this connection, all outsiders are to be looked upon as strangers—not merely Americans, but Canadians, English, Irish and Scotch. All are strangers in the sense that they are outsiders, that they do not appreciate the circumstances in which we live and are not likely to enter fully into our views and feelings."

Riel's characterization of newcomers as "strangers" shocked James Ross, who criticized the Métis leader's seemingly protectionist views. "I am very much astonished that Mr. Riel, who is working for the people of this country, should make such a speech," he said. The exchange between Riel and Ross highlighted the contrasting perspectives of French and English delegates at the convention. As Red River prepared for mass settlement from the east, primarily from English-speaking Ontario, French-speaking Métis were far more concerned about being "swamped" by newcomers, or "strangers," as Riel called them, than their English-speaking counterparts.

John A. Macdonald lent some credence to Riel's concerns. It was clear the prime minister envisioned precisely what Riel feared. In a letter to a friend in October 1869, Macdonald wrote: "It will require considerable management to keep those wild people quiet [in Red River]. In another year the present residents will be altogether swamped by the influx of strangers who will go in with the idea of becoming industrious and peaceable settlers."[18]

The demand for immediate provincial status wasn't the only change made to the list of rights following the Convention of Forty deliberations. A request for separate denominational schools, including public funding based on population, was also added. Like the provincial status addition, it is unclear who made the change, although it is thought to have been influenced by Bishop Taché, who had returned to Red River following his trip to Rome and before the delegates left for Ottawa.

Meanwhile, the question of who would govern Red River until negotiations with the federal government were completed still had to be addressed. It was agreed on February 10 by the Convention of Forty that a renewed, elected government made up of twelve French and twelve English members would be formed (later expanded to twenty-eight members), with several officers and a president appointed by the convention. A two-thirds vote of the new assembly would overrule the veto of the president. Thus, the first elected legislative assembly in Red River was created. It was the second provisional government declared during the resistance, this time with the support and participation of English-speaking delegates.

However, that support did not come immediately. English-speaking delegates were still hesitant to endorse a provisional government for many of the same reasons they opposed it in November. This time they sought the approval of a higher authority. They found that approval in a very ill and bedridden William Mactavish, the HBC governor who was still living at Upper Fort Garry and whose health was deteriorating (he would die in July 1870). Two English delegates—John Fraser and John Sutherland from the Kildonan parish—paid the governor a visit to seek his guidance. "I asked his opinion as to the advisability of forming a provisional government," Sutherland told the convention. "He replied, 'Form a government for God's sake and restore peace and order in the settlement.'" Sutherland's announcement prompted cheers from the convention.

With the governor's blessing, the English-speaking delegates were now prepared to join their French countrymen in declaring a provisional gov-

[18] Letter from John A. Macdonald to friend J.Y. Bown, Oct. 14, 1869. Lionel Dorge, "Bishop Taché and the Confederation of Manitoba, 1869–1870," *MHS Transactions*, Series 3, Number 26, 1969–70 season, Manitoba Historical Society Archives. Accessed Apr. 23, 2024, https://www.mhs.mb.ca/docs/transactions/3/tacheconfederation.shtml.

ernment. Without Mactavish's endorsement, some delegates had feared that establishing a provisional government might be interpreted as disloyalty to the British Crown. Many French-speaking Métis had held the same apprehensions in November when the first provisional government was proposed. Again, Riel had to convince them that protecting their political rights would not compromise their status as British subjects.

James Ross expounded on Mactavish's endorsement the following day as justification for declaring a provisional government. "The man in this country who has—if anybody has—legal authority, authority from England, has told us plainly that for his part, we are at perfect liberty to go forward and form any government we think best for the welfare of the country," he told the convention, prompting more cheers. "I am glad we have got rid of that difficulty. It relieves our people at one stroke from a sense of responsibility which they felt to be weighing them down to the ground."

Mactavish had no authority to delegate such powers to anyone. But it was enough to give the English speakers clear consciences to proceed, or at least enough political cover to defend themselves should anyone question their decision in the future. Either way, an important political union was established that would strengthen their bargaining power with the federal government at the negotiating table. For the first time since the beginning of the resistance, the French- and English-speaking sectors were politically united.

The matter of electing a president was next. Riel was the clear front-runner and was nominated for the top spot. Some English representatives questioned whether they had the mandate of their constituents to authorize such an appointment, prompting more debate. An agitated Riel wondered aloud why the English delegates were present if they could not make decisions on behalf of their people. After several representatives rose in support of Riel, including Ross, the Métis leader was chosen president. The *New Nation* newspaper reported on the outcome:

> The confirmation of Louis Riel as President of the Provisional Government of Rupert's Land, by the Convention, was announced amid salvos or artillery from the Fort and the cheers of the delegates. The Town welcomed the announcements by a grand display of

> fireworks and the general and continued discharge of small arms. The firing and cheering were prolonged until late in the night, everyone joining in general enthusiasm. As a result of the amicable union of all parties upon one common platform, a general amnesty to political prisoners will shortly be claimed, the soldiers remanded to their homes to await orders and everything be placed upon a peace footing. "Vive la Republique."[19]

Most of the twenty-four parishes elected members to the new legislative assembly within days, but not all. Some English-speaking parishes did not immediately consent. Once they did, the new Legislative Assembly of Assiniboia sat from March 9 to June 24, 1870, in the courthouse. It was a historic moment for the settlement, a precursor to the provincial status they would soon enjoy, including an elected legislative assembly under the Dominion of Canada. It was the Red River Settlement's first taste of responsible government.

"We have worked here in the past in anxiety and fear," Riel said in his opening address to the legislative assembly on its first day of sitting. "But we have worked conscientiously. That the majority, at least, have done so, I fully believe. One result of our labours is that the people generally now have, for the first time in the history of this land, a voice in the direction of public affairs. They have here a full representation."[20]

The provisional legislative assembly governed the community until Manitoba officially joined Canada later that year. It approved several bills, including some related to public works and land titles. A revised list of rights was presented to the assembly, which included the controversial demand for provincial status, although there is no record of debate on it.

---

19 *New Nation*, supplement, Feb. 11, 1870. *Vive la Republique* means "long live the republic." The governance model chosen by the people of Red River was a presidential one, perhaps U.S.-influenced, which included the separation of the executive and legislative branches of government, in contrast to the British parliamentary system adopted by Canada, and later Manitoba, where the executive (premiers and cabinet ministers) typically sit as members of the legislature.

20 *New Nation*, Mar. 11, 1870.

The people of Red River were under no illusion that the new governing body would continue once Manitoba joined Canada. It was understood that, under Confederation, a new form of government would take its place. Riel told the assembly that he would "give up his place willingly and joyfully as President as soon as a proper governor came."[21] During debates in the house, when discussing the issue of drafting a new constitution, Riel reminded members that the legislative assembly was a temporary form of government. "We are only a Provisional body, but it seems to me that it would be well to show, in the way proposed, what are the aims of the present Government," he said.[22] In June, Riel spoke enthusiastically about an expected peaceful transfer of power with the arrival of a new lieutenant-governor from Ottawa, under terms delegates from Red River negotiated with the federal government. "For myself, it will be my duty and pleasure, more than any other, to bid the new governor welcome on his arrival," Riel told the legislative assembly, prompting cheers from members. "I would like to be the first to pay him the respect due to his position as representative of the Crown."[23]

Despite the setbacks and underlying tensions that remained in the settlement, the people of Red River were moving in near unison towards a negotiated settlement with Canada. They had come a long way since the Métis expelled federal surveyors from their land and prevented William McDougall from entering the settlement. Victory was within reach; they would join Canada, but under their terms.

The people of Red River were also adopting new democratic institutions. Notwithstanding Riel's occasional bouts of autocratic rule, most of the decisions made in preparation for negotiations with Ottawa were adopted through elected bodies. That level of democracy had not existed in Red River prior to the resistance (at least not since colonial rule), other than the democratic principles used by the Métis during buffalo hunts. Red

---

21 *Alexander Begg's Red River Journal*, entry from Mar. 15, 1870, 337. The *New Nation* also reported this on Mar. 18, 1870.

22 *New Nation*, Apr. 2, 1870.

23 *New Nation*, July 1, 1870.

River as a community had been governed by the Hudson's Bay Company and an appointed Council of Assiniboia prior to the events of 1869–70. Until then, there had been no elected government in Rupert's Land.

There was, for the first time in many weeks, a sense of good things to come in Red River. "In the town of Winnipeg brilliant fireworks were set off and bonfires lighted—guns fired and cheering and drinking universal," Begg wrote in his journal. "A regular drunk commenced in which everyone seemed to join."[24] Louis Schmidt, who was later elected to the Legislative Assembly of Manitoba, recalled in his memoirs the sense of optimism many felt at the time: "The evening which followed that happy outcome was one of gaiety and rejoicing. Bonfires were lighted and it was one of the few good times that were spent in the Fort."[25]

---

[24] *Alexander Begg's Red River Journal*, entry for Feb. 10, 1870, 303.

[25] "Memoirs of Louis Schmidt," 473.

CHAPTER 3

...

The Execution of Thomas Scott

ARBITRARY IMPRISONMENT occurred on a regular basis in Red River in the fall and winter of 1869–70. No due process or judicial principles guaranteed an individual's presumption of innocence before guilt was proven in a court of law. There were no bail hearings or anything resembling bail court. Even the Quarterly Court that existed in Red River prior to the resistance was suspended for about two months during the height of the armed conflict. For the most part, Riel and the Métis were the police, judge and jury when it came to arresting and jailing their enemies—or perceived enemies—at Upper Fort Garry. They did so frequently. Even a hint of insubordination or a perceived threat against the provisional government was grounds for detention. It wasn't unusual to have thirty, forty or fifty political prisoners locked up at any given time. Those captured were often released with a promise not to disturb the peace (the closest thing to bail), or a pledge not to challenge the authority of the provisional government. At least 114 people were incarcerated at Fort Garry during the resistance, many of whom were locked up for a month or more. That was the number recorded who received financial compensation from the federal government in 1871 after Manitoba joined Canada. There may have been more who spent time in the makeshift prison cells who did not submit a claim.

John Christian Schultz was one of those political prisoners. Schultz, a white man who came to Red River from Ontario in 1861 in anticipation of annexation, led a group of Canadian Loyalists opposed to Riel's regime. He was a polarizing figure in the settlement. His acrimonious relationship with the Métis—and with Riel in particular—underscored the persecution Indigenous people faced from non-Indigenous newcomers as Canada made plans to annex the territory. Schultz's "Canadian Party," as he called it, supported joining Canada unconditionally, in large part because it could then exploit the territory to its benefit while marginalizing and displacing the people who lived there. By 1869, a small number of Canadians from Ontario had already emigrated to Red River in anticipation of western expansion. Many hoped to get a jump on land acquisition, expecting property values to rise dramatically once Rupert's Land joined Confederation. Schultz and his supporters had been politically active in the settlement for several years, not only to promote Canadian annexation, but also to challenge the Hudson's Bay Company's political monopoly over the region, which they saw as a threat to their interests. They published the only newspaper in Red River at the time, the *Nor'Wester* (which was eventually shut down by Riel), to advance their political agenda prior to the resistance.

Schultz and his group not only opposed the Métis and their provisional government, they were openly hostile towards them. Racial and religious tensions drove much of the conflict during the resistance, a divide that would deepen with the influx of white settlers and the arrival of British troops and Canadian militia the following year. Schultz's Canadian Party was determined to remove whatever barriers it perceived stood in the way of Canadian annexation, even if that meant trampling on the rights of local inhabitants. For that, they found themselves behind bars at Fort Garry on a regular basis following the declaration of the first provisional government. Riel and his supporters saw Schultz and the Canadian Party as a threat to their very existence. "They had often spoken of undertaking to chase the *métis* as far as the Rocky Mountains in order to rid the environs of Fort Garry of their presence," Riel wrote in his memoirs.[1]

Mass arrests were not uncommon in Red River during the resistance. One of the largest occurred in December 1869 after an armed standoff between the Métis and a group of about forty Schultz supporters who barricaded themselves in his home in the village of Winnipeg.[2] Schultz had stored pork and other provisions for the federal government in the store attached to his house (to supply workers on the Dawson Road project near Lake of the Woods). The Canadians were concerned that the Métis might seize the goods because supplies were getting low in the settlement. As a precaution, Schultz had organized a group of volunteers to guard the provisions. Riel and the Métis perceived the move as an act of hostility. They also suspected Schultz's group was planning an attack on the fort. In response, they surrounded the home with guns drawn. The standoff lasted hours and had the potential to turn into a bloodbath. Luckily, cooler heads prevailed. After lengthy negotiations, Schultz and his supporters—outmanned and outgunned—agreed to a peaceful surrender. No shots were fired and it was agreed no women would be arrested. The remainder were marched off to jail at Upper Fort Garry.

James H. Ashdown, who became a prominent member of the business community in Winnipeg after Manitoba joined Canada, was among those taken prisoner from the Schultz store. He was locked up with twenty-two other people on the second floor of a two-storey building in office space normally occupied by HBC accountants and clerks. The ventilation in the twelve- by thirty-six-foot room was so poor that the prisoners were forced to break a window to get fresh air. Ashdown and several others arrested that day were locked up for more than two months. He would later recount the harrowing experience in a *Manitoba Free Press* story. "The French half-breeds were no tender jailers," the newspaper reported in its 1919 feature story on Ashdown. "The bill of fare consisted of pemmican and tea. Had it

1 "Memoir by Louis Riel on the Course and Purpose of the Red River Resistance, Written in 1874," in *Alexander Begg's Red River Journal and Other Papers Relative to the Red River Resistance of 1869–70*, edited by W.L. Morton (Toronto: The Champlain Society, 1956), 532.

2 The "village" or "town" of Winnipeg, as it was called prior to its incorporation in 1873, was situated in what is today the Exchange District of downtown Winnipeg. See map on page 14.

not been for the kindness of women in the village and the good offices of Joseph Crowson, who, on account of lameness was suffered to go at large by Riel and who carried provisions to the fort, the prisoners would have almost starved. As it was, many of the good things intended for them were snatched out of Crowson's baskets by the half-breed bandits."[3]

The federal government established a commission in the summer of 1871, a year after Manitoba joined Confederation (around the same time First Nations negotiated Treaty 1 at Lower Fort Garry), to pay compensation to those who claimed losses during the resistance. Close to two hundred people submitted claims to commissioner Francis G. Johnson totaling $336,261 for loss of property, damages, imprisonment and "forced emigration." A fraction of that, $85,756, was paid out. Some claims were denied; most were reduced. The majority of the 161 people who received compensation had English names, although some were French.

John Schultz received the largest settlement at $34,890, of which $31,890 was for loss of property and $3,000 for imprisonment and forced emigration. Anyone who could convince the commissioner that they had been forced to flee Red River during the resistance for fear of personal safety was eligible for compensation. Joseph Monkman, an English-speaking Métis and an ally of Schultz (he helped the latter escape Red River and travel to eastern Canada in 1870), was paid $500 for forced emigration.

Most claimants incarcerated by Riel received $2 in compensation for each day they spent locked up. Some of those who served longer sentences were awarded $4 per day, presumably to reflect the added hardship of their loss of freedom. One A.J. Dilworth was awarded $160 for "4 months, at $40 per month," for imprisonment. Alfred Boyd, Manitoba's first provincial secretary in 1870, received $2,509, the second-largest settlement, for "value of guns seized by insurgents." James H. Ashdown was paid $140 for seventy days' imprisonment and Charles Mair from Portage la Prairie received $1,976 for sixty-eight days in prison.[4]

Among those taken into custody at the Schultz home in December was

---

[3] *Manitoba Free Press*, Sept. 11, 1919.

[4] "Compensation to the Sufferers During the Insurrection in Rupert's Land," House of Commons sessional papers, 1872, vol. 6, no. 19, 5–7.

Thomas Scott, an Orangeman[5] from Ontario who had come to Red River to work on the Dawson Road construction project, a route that would eventually connect northwestern Ontario to Manitoba. Schultz, Scott and others escaped captivity a few weeks later. It is believed Schultz used a pen-knife smuggled in by his wife during a visit to dig his way through a window frame at the fort. After removing the frame, he scaled a wall to freedom, injuring himself in the process. Schultz remained in hiding for weeks, avoiding rearrest. Riel ordered him shot on sight if found. The chief nemesis of the Métis would later enjoy a successful career in Canadian politics, including winning a seat in the House of Commons and serving in the Canadian Senate. He was appointed Manitoba's fifth lieutenant-governor in 1888.

Two months after his first arrest, Thomas Scott was captured and imprisoned again. This time he would not escape, nor would he emerge alive.

By February 1870, the people of Red River had made significant progress towards finding a peaceful resolution to their troubles. They were on a path towards a negotiated settlement with Canada and were eager to enjoy the benefits of joining Confederation. But that relative peace was shattered after a botched coup organized by Schultz and his supporters. Despite the success of the Convention of Forty, or perhaps because of it, the Canadian Party planned an attack on Upper Fort Garry in mid-February. They sought the immediate release of all prisoners and planned to install a provisional government of their own.

A large group of Schultz supporters travelled from Portage la Prairie (about 50 miles west of Winnipeg) to the parish of Kildonan on the cold early morning of February 17. The plan was to amass an armed regiment of a few hundred men to take the fort. However, the campaign was doomed to failure from the start. Schultz and his men were disorganized, ill-equipped and suffered from poor leadership. The planned attack was abandoned soon after the men reached Kildonan.

Charles Mair, a member of the Schultz group, would later blame the

---

[5] The Orange Order was an anti-Catholic and anti-French political and religious organization that promoted Protestantism and emphasized its allegiance to the British monarchy and its colonial governments.

"Scotch settlers" in Red River "who refused to rise and march on Fort Garry, which, had they shown more determination, could easily have been captured."[6] It was evident, though, that the lack of an organized and properly equipped offensive was the underlying cause of the failed coup.

Schultz, still a wanted man by Riel, abandoned the failed mission but it is unclear at what point he fled. Most of the others either dropped out along the way or returned home. What remained was a group of forty-seven detractors who walked within eyesight of Fort Garry on their way back to Portage. Meanwhile, Riel and the Métis had gotten word of the planned attack and had a defensive strategy in place. When they spotted the would-be insurgents near the fort, they deployed a squad of armed horsemen to apprehend them. The group was arrested without incident. No shots were fired.

Among those captured was Thomas Scott, his second imprisonment after escaping in January. He was among five prisoners condemned to death, including Charles Boulton, one of the principal leaders of the failed coup. However, four of the five, including Boulton, were pardoned by Riel after persistent lobbying by several clergy and leaders in the community.

Riel may have used Boulton's planned execution as a bargaining chip to encourage several English-speaking parishes, which had still not elected members to the new legislative assembly, to nominate candidates and show support for the provisional government. According to HBC governor William Mactavish, Riel said he would spare Boulton's life if those parishes elected representatives to the assembly. The Métis leader enlisted Donald A. Smith, who agreed to Riel's conditions, to canvass residents of those parishes and get them onside. "[Smith] visited the various districts referred to, and finally the number of English delegates required to complete the 'Legislative Council' were elected and returned," wrote Mactavish.[7]

---

6 *Daily British Whig*, Kingston, Ontario, Apr. 9, 1870. Mair made the comments during an "indignation meeting" in Toronto, where Schultz and his supporters were stirring up anti-Riel sentiment.

7 Letter from William Mactavish to W.G. Smith, secretary of the Hudson's Bay Company, Apr. 6, 1870, House of Commons sessional papers, 1871, vol. 5, no. 44, 27.

Thomas Scott would get no such mercy. He was tried and convicted by a military tribunal on March 3 for rebelling against the provisional government and attacking a Métis guard at Upper Fort Garry. The trial, overseen by Métis adjutant-general Ambroise Lépine, was not conducted under normal court rules, even by 1870 Red River standards. Scott had no defence counsel and was not present for most of the proceedings, which were mainly conducted in French (a language the Irish-born Canadian did not understand). Riel, one of the chief witnesses in the case, acted as translator. The military council found Scott guilty and sentenced him to death. However, the sentencing decision was not unanimous. Some members of the tribunal felt the penalty was too harsh.

The Scott trial and subsequent execution would forever change the complexion of the Red River Resistance. Riel and his supporters would face severe and persistent criticism, not only for how Scott's trial was carried out but over whether the provisional government even had the jurisdiction to conduct such a legal proceeding. "Even the decencies of an ordinary drumhead court martial were disregarded," wrote Lord Dufferin, Canada's governor general in 1875. "The trial, if it can be so termed, was conducted in the absence of the accused, who was confronted with no witnesses, nor furnished with any indictment, nor allowed to plead for his life."[8]

News of the death sentence spread like wildfire throughout the settlement. Several prominent members of the community attempted to convince Riel to spare Scott's life, as they had with the four other prisoners sentenced to death. Executing political prisoners who opposed the provisional government was seen by many as rash, cruel and entirely unnecessary under the circumstances. But Riel wouldn't budge. The Métis leader was committed to carrying it through, regardless of the consequences. Why did Riel choose to execute Scott and not the others? Why any of them? Nothing in the literature conclusively answers those questions.

A bewildered Scott, who initially thought the planned execution was an empty threat, was escorted outside the east-side walls of Upper Fort Garry

[8] Correspondence from Lord Dufferin to Earl of Carnarvon, Britain's secretary of state for the colonies, Dec. 4, 1874, House of Commons sessional papers, 1875, vol. 7, no. 11, 12.

at noon on March 4, then blindfolded and shot by a firing squad. According to some eyewitnesses—about one hundred bystanders arrived at the fort after hearing about the planned execution—Scott did not immediately die after he was shot by the firing squad, and one of his executioners was forced to shoot him at close range with a revolver. Alexander Begg described the execution in his journal: "Scott was then brought out—it is said he prayed as he walked—a bandage was then put over his eyes and he knelt . . . Scott fell forward, pierced in four places—he was not dead yet but struggled on the ground."[9] Scott was then placed in a makeshift wooden coffin and brought back inside the fort.

Countless rumours and much speculation circulated over how the execution was carried out, including whether members of the firing squad had been consuming alcohol at the time. Many of the eyewitness accounts were contradictory. Scott's time of death and the possibility that he remained alive for several hours after the execution was never settled. Even the whereabouts of his body remains a mystery. Some reports had him buried on the grounds of Upper Fort Garry. Others said several Métis cut a hole in the ice of a nearby river and secretly dumped his body there. Riel, in an interview with a Winnipeg newspaper thirteen years later, said Scott's body might have been dumped in the river, but he didn't know. "I have always declined to answer that question," said Riel. "It might have been, but I am not supposed to know, and in fact don't know."[10]

Based on reports that Scott may have been buried inside the walls of Upper Fort Garry, local officials attempted to exhume his body several months later, after the arrival in 1870 of Manitoba's first lieutenant-governor, Adams Archibald. The "excavation" of what was believed to be Scott's body took place in front of a small group of officials, including Archibald. *The Manitoban* newspaper reported on it at the time:

> As the hole deepened, the excitement became the more intense, and when, after digging some six feet, the spade struck on a board, and when the earth was removed and disclosed a deal board shaped like a

---

[9] *Alexander Begg's Red River Journal*, entry from March 4, 1870, 328.

[10] *Winnipeg Daily Sun*, June 29, 1883.

> coffin, every one held his breath. But the excitement was turned into something like disappointed rage when one of the diggers thrust his arm into the box and pronounced it empty! It was empty, and there was no other box there; and where the remains of poor Thomas Scott have been bestowed will probably never be known.[11]

Scott's execution had a profound effect on the settlement. Until then, dozens of people had been taken prisoner, but none had faced such a severe punishment. It was the first time blood was shed during the Red River Resistance, at least as it related directly to the armed uprising. "A deep gloom has settled over the settlement on account of this deed," wrote Begg in his journal.[12]

A week later, during his first sermon since returning to Red River from Rome, Bishop Alexandre Taché pleaded with his parishioners (including Riel, who was among the worshippers at the St. Boniface Cathedral) "to use charity and forbearance to each other and to act in union together." It was an emotional time in Red River. Taché, who had great influence in the community, told his parishioners that Canada would do right by them and that it was time for the people of the settlement to come together. "He said he loved all Catholics and Protestants and would like to see all working in harmony," Begg wrote. "Bishop Taché was very much affected during portions of his address and the greater part of those who heard him shed tears while he spoke. Riel was in the church and it is said was very much affected during the sermon—shedding tears at times."[13]

Meanwhile, the Legislative Assembly of Assiniboia held its first sitting on March 9, five days after Scott's execution. If the death of Scott affected the mood of the proceedings, it was not evident in the members' speeches. Taché was introduced to the assembly upon his return to the settlement. He had made a stop in Ottawa on his way back from Rome after cutting short his stay there. The federal government had formally requested the bishop's return to Red River to help quell the "troubles" in the settlement.

---

11 *The Manitoban*, October 15, 1870.

12 *Alexander Begg's Red River Journal*, entry from March 4, 1870, 328.

13 *Alexander Begg's Red River Journal*, entry from March 13, 1870, 335.

Taché offered a message of hope to the assembly. "I can well understand the anxiety of the people, at the crisis in public affairs with which we have to deal," he told the assembly. "I believe it to be an anxiety deep and widespread. Let me express the hope, however, that all feeling of this kind will cease. It is a hope grounded on my own conviction that this anxiety is now needless, and that a brighter and better day will speedily dawn on this land." His speech prompted cheers from members.[14]

No single event during the Red River Resistance has attracted more debate and commentary from scholars and historians than the death of Thomas Scott. Many saw his execution as a grave error that could have been avoided. The killing has been described as illegal and morally reprehensible. A newspaper in the east called it "barbaric" and "one of the most despicable human butcheries that has taken place in a civilized community for a length of time."[15] Others saw it as a necessary step to maintain order in the settlement and to demonstrate to the federal government and others that the provisional government had political legitimacy. If Scott, who was relentlessly abusive towards Métis guards while in captivity (Riel later claimed Scott tried to kill a guard with a bayonet[16]), had not been executed through some form of tribunal, it was possible he might have been murdered by guards. It was, perhaps, what Riel was trying to avoid. The Métis leader would later write: "The boldness of our enemies, however, encouraged by our patience, had become extreme. It even broke out among the prisoners of war that we had taken on February 17, even within the walls of Fort Garry. It was necessary to put an end to all of that. It was necessary to inflict a condign punishment on the plotters and madmen."[17]

Although he didn't mention Scott by name, it appears Riel justified the killing in a proclamation he wrote just over two months after the execution. He referred to those who "continued to trouble the public peace," which "forced us to make an example of him [presumably Scott] by which others might learn."[18]

---

[14] *New Nation*, Mar. 16, 1870.

[15] *Canadian Statesman*, Bowmanville, Ontario, Apr. 14, 1870.

[16] Riel interview, *Winnipeg Daily Sun*, June 29, 1883.

[17] "Memoir by Louis Riel," *Alexander Begg's Red River Journal*, 540.

According to Donald A. Smith, Riel told him the execution was necessary to ensure Canada took the provisional government seriously. If true, it had the opposite effect. The killing of Scott made it more difficult for Red River delegates to negotiate a favourable deal with officials in Ottawa the following month. Louis Schmidt, a member of both provisional governments, wrote the following in his memoirs: "I shall not pause to try to justify that execution, which the people of Ontario have used for such a long time to raise prejudice and hatred, not only against the Métis but against all that is French and Catholic. I believe that today all impartial men grant that Riel and his government were perfectly right to act as they did."[19]

Historian Maggie Siggins, in her biography *Riel: A Life of Revolution*, wrote: "Almost every historian over the years has condemned the execution of Thomas Scott as being without any legal foundation. But the Métis and Riel believed the government was a legitimate one, invested with the power to mete out justice and impose the death penalty if need be."

The British government saw it differently. Henry Herbert, the Earl of Carnarvon and Britain's colonial secretary, was adamant that the provisional government was neither legitimate nor had the legal authority to execute Scott. "That the murderers of Scott represented a de facto government, and are consequently excusable on political grounds, is one which I cannot for a moment entertain," he wrote. "There could be within the Queen's possessions in North America no power or pretence of establishing a *de facto* government, independent of, or defying her Majesty and Her officers, which could aspire to any such immunity as that claimed; and any argument based on the view of such a state of things being possible, is in my opinion not even worthy of discussion."[20]

Lord Dufferin echoed those views: "It is very evident that the killing of

---

18 Proclamation issued by Riel, May 14, 1870, reprinted in *Alexander Begg's Red River Journal*, 525.

19 "Memoirs of Louis Schmidt," in *Alexander Begg's Red River Journal*, 474.

20 Letter from the Earl of Carnarvon to Lord Dufferin, governor general of Canada, Jan. 7, 1875, House of Commons sessional paper, 1875, vol. 7, no. 11, 38. Britain was asked for its input on the commutation of Ambroise Lépine's sentence, since the execution of Scott occurred prior to Manitoba's entry into Canada.

Scott was not an exercise of jurisdiction known to any form of law, but an inhuman slaughter of an innocent man, aggravated by circumstances of extraordinary brutality," he wrote in 1874. "The utmost alleged against Scott is that he used violent language in prison, and that he had alluded to an intention of capturing Riel and retaining him as a hostage for the release of the prisoners already referred to; but even these allegations were not proved, nor, had they been proved ten times over, could they have rendered him liable to serious punishment."[21]

Whatever the case, Scott's death not only made it more difficult for Red River delegates to negotiate in Ottawa, it had a profound impact on Riel's future. The Métis leader fled Red River in late August when a military expedition sent by the federal government, many of whose soldiers were intent on capturing the "murderers of Scott," arrived from Ontario. He became a fugitive for years after the resistance and was unable to take his seat in Parliament after he was elected three times as an MP, fearing arrest, death or other forms of reprisal.

Ambroise Lépine was the only person convicted for Scott's death, four years after the resistance.[22] Lépine was sentenced to death in 1875, but his sentence was commuted to two years in prison with the forfeiture of his political rights. The latter was on the recommendation of Britain, whose advice the federal government sought since Red River was not part of Canada when Scott's execution took place. The Earl of Carnarvon wrote, "I should not therefore think it unreasonable, while it would undoubtedly conduce to a higher tone of constitutional morality, that the liberation of the criminals after the expiration of their commuted sentence, should be accompanied by some stringent conditions as to their good conduct, if they remain in any part of Canada, and by their total exclusion from any participation in political or parliamentary life."[23]

---

21 Lord Dufferin to the Earl of Carnarvon, Dec. 4, 1874, 12.

22 André Nault, a French Métis who played a significant role in the resistance and was part of the tribunal that convicted Scott, was also prosecuted for Scott's death. However, the jury could not reach a verdict in his case and he was eventually set free under a general amnesty in 1875.

23 Earl of Carnarvon to Lord Dufferin, Jan. 7, 1875, 40.

The colonial secretary also expressed displeasure with Riel's election to the House of Commons[24] even though the Métis leader never took his seat in Parliament. "It has been a source of much pain to many who, like myself, take pride in the public institutions of Canada, to hear of the legislature being disgraced by the election to the House of Commons and the presence within its walls of a criminal like Riel."[25]

Lord Dufferin authorized the commutation of Lépine's sentence. He said that while most people in Ontario viewed Riel as a "disloyal rebel" and a "murderer" and would consider Riel's and Lépine's escape from punishment as a "miscarriage of justice," there was also some appetite for leniency. "At the same time the larger proportion of them feel that various circumstances have occurred to complicate the situation, and to render the capital sentence impossible of execution," he wrote, "and even amongst the more extreme section of those who are animated by sentiments of intense sympathy for Scott, there is to be observed, as far as I can judge from the newspapers, a moderation and reasonableness which does them considerable credit."[26]

The views of parliamentarians on the actions of Riel and his supporters were decidedly (and not unexpectedly) mixed. During a House of Commons debate in 1874 on whether to grant a general amnesty to those who participated in the resistance, a young Wilfred Laurier—the MP for Drummond-Arthabaska and a future Canadian prime minister—offered a lengthy and convincing defence of Riel and the Métis:

> It has also been said that Mr. Riel was only a rebel. How was it possible to use such language? What act of rebellion did he commit? Did he ever raise any other standard than the national flag? Did he ever proclaim any other authority than the sovereign authority of the Queen? No, never. His whole crime and the crime of his friends was that they

[24] Riel was first elected to the House of Commons in a by-election in 1873 in the constituency of Provencher. He was twice re-elected in the riding, but never took his seat in Parliament.

[25] Earl of Carnarvon to Lord Dufferin, Jan. 7, 1875, 40.

[26] Letter from Lord Dufferin to the Earl of Carnarvon, Dec. 10, 1874, House of Commons sessional papers, 1875, vol. 7, no. 11, 15.

> wanted to be treated like British subjects and not to be bartered away like common cattle? If that be an act of rebellion, where is the one amongst us, who, if he had happened to have been with them, would not have been rebels as they were? Taken all in all, I would regard the events at Red River in 1869–70 as constituting a glorious page in our history, if unfortunately they had not been stained with the blood of Thomas Scott. But such is the state of human nature and of all that is human: good and evil are constantly intermingled; the most glorious cause is not free from impurity and the vilest may have its noble side.[27]

Alive, Thomas Scott would barely warrant a footnote in the story of the Red River Resistance. Dead, he became a martyr for an anti-Métis cause in eastern Canada that changed the course of Manitoba history. Had Scott not been executed, Red River delegates might have had more leverage at the bargaining table in Ottawa when negotiating the Manitoba Act. Riel almost certainly would have been able to assume a formal role in Manitoba and Canadian politics after the province joined Confederation.

Despite Scott's death and the impact it had on the community, there was renewed hope in the spring of 1870 that the delegates sent to Ottawa would negotiate a favourable deal for the people of Red River. Riel published a proclamation in the *New Nation* newspaper on April 9, 1870, that read in part: "Canada invites the Red River people to an amicable arrangement. She offers to guarantee us our rights and to give us a place in the Confederation equal to that of any other province."[28] There was cautious optimism in the air.

Still, much effort was required to restore peace and stability in the settle-

---

[27] House of Commons debate, 3rd Parliament, 1st Session, vol. I, Apr. 15, 1874, https://thecanadianencyclopedia.ca/en/article/wilfrid-laurier-speech-in-defence-of-louis-riel-1874.

[28] At the time this proclamation was published, the federal government had not yet agreed to allow Manitoba to enter Canada with provincial status. That would not occur until later that month during negotiations in Ottawa between the delegates, Prime Minister John A. Macdonald and George-Étienne Cartier, the federal minister of militia and defence.

ment. A key part of achieving that was to restore economic activity in the region. That included persuading the Hudson's Bay Company—the main economic engine of Red River—to resume business after a winter of stalled operations. It would be no easy task. In a letter to company officials, HBC governor William Mactavish said resuming operations was rife with logistical challenges after the Métis had spent months pilfering the company's inventory and supplies.

> Fort Garry had been entirely taken from our hand by the French half-breeds party, the leaders of which had with violence seized the keys of all the shops, stores and warehouses within its walls, and have for months past been carrying away the company's property of all kinds in vast quantities without let or hindrance. As you are aware a large quantity of valuable furs have remained in store here since last autumn. These along with everything else have been seized, and we find ourselves perfectly powerless to repossess ourselves of them, without the permission of Riel and his people. Our servants have been expelled from their houses and obliged to live outside the Fort, to provide accommodation for the half-breeds.[29]

Riel wanted the HBC to resume operations but only under certain conditions, which he presented to Mactavish in writing. One of his conditions was that the HBC would have to lend the provisional government £3,000 sterling and an additional £2,000 if talks with Canada fell through. HBC would also have to agree to supply the "military department" of the provisional government with £4,000 worth of merchandise. "On accepting these conditions the company shall open its stores under the protection of the Provisional Government," wrote Riel. "Fort Garry shall be opened, remaining at the same time the seat of Government under a small guard of fifty men. Such, sir, are the conditions which the situation imposes upon us. I shall not shrink from the performance of my duty; you have a proper sense of your own, and I am confident your decision will be favourable."[30]

Mactavish, whose health continued to deteriorate, had little choice but

[29] Mactavish to Smith, Apr. 6, 1870, 28.

to accept Riel's terms. He said it was critical for the HBC to resume operations. "I feel that my compliance with their demands, on behalf of the company, affords our only chance of avoiding immediate, inevitable destruction," wrote Mactavish. "We hope to be able to carry on our summer trade, but in consequence of the dreadful pillage we have sustained we shall do so in a very crippled condition."[31]

The stage was now set for the next chapter of Manitoba's entry into Canada: face-to-face negotiations with the federal government.

---

[30] Mactavish to Smith, Apr. 6, 1870, 30. Mactavish quoted Riel's letter and conditions in his letter to W.G. Smith.

[31] Mactavish to Smith, Apr. 6, 1870, 28–29.

CHAPTER 4

. . .

The Ottawa Negotiations

NOËL-JOSEPH RITCHOT had the most important job in the Red River Settlement in the spring of 1870. The St. Norbert parish priest was about to go toe-to-toe with the most powerful politicians in Ottawa—John A. Macdonald, Canada's prime minister, and his right-hand man, George-Étienne Cartier, the federal minister of militia and defence. Ritchot, a French Canadian who had moved to Red River in 1862, was one of three delegates chosen by the provisional government at Upper Fort Garry to negotiate the terms of Manitoba's entry into Confederation. He did not speak English and had no formal experience in politics, much less a background in constitutional law. However, the man with the long black beard, at age forty-five, found himself as the principal negotiator for the Red River Settlement, more out of necessity than personal desire. Whether he knew it or not at the time, the fate of the settlement—and the future of Manitoba—rested on his shoulders.

Ritchot was an influential figure in the early stages of the Red River Resistance who lent his moral support to the French-speaking Métis. Many of those who followed his guidance, including Louis Riel, were his parishioners. He was an important political and spiritual advisor to the Métis and an obvious choice as their chosen delegate. Judge John Black, the head of the General Quarterly Court of Assiniboia, was chosen as the anglophone representative. Black had played a key role in the Convention of Forty and was a respected public figure in the community. He initially declined the nomination but was later persuaded by Bishop Taché to accept the appointment.

Black had frequently been at odds with Riel during the Convention of Forty deliberations. He was similarly unsupportive of Ritchot at times during negotiations in Ottawa. For the most part, though, he took a back seat to Ritchot during talks with the federal government. He appeared to have had little impact on the outcome of the talks. Ritchot led most of the negotiations, including pressing Ottawa on key demands, many of which were eventually adopted by Parliament.

Alfred Scott—a bartender and a store clerk in the village of Winnipeg—was the third delegate, selected to represent the interests of the small group of Americans living in the community. Scott (no relation to Thomas Scott) played almost no role in the negotiations in Ottawa, at least none that have been documented.

Some delegates had suggested during the Convention of Forty deliberations that Riel should be one of the representatives sent to Ottawa to negotiate with federal officials. He was, after all, the undisputed leader of the resistance and likely the most capable of negotiating the best terms for his people, particularly the French Métis. He would have been the only Indigenous delegate at the negotiating table, fitting since Rupert's Land was populated mainly by Métis and First Nations people. However, Riel declined. He told the convention his role was to remain in Red River to fulfil his duties as president of the provisional government. Besides, since the execution of Thomas Scott and the anti-Riel campaign it had triggered in eastern Canada, it was out of the question for the Métis leader to travel to Ottawa. It would have been virtually impossible to assure his safety, and his presence in Ontario would have been a major distraction during negotiations, making it difficult to hold productive talks.

Ritchot was the clear leader among the delegates. The parish priest was chosen for his persistence, intellectual capacity and loyalty to the Métis cause. He had no experience bartering with high-powered politicians, but his dogged determination and a natural political skill set he probably didn't know he had made him a formidable opponent at the negotiating table.

Ritchot left Red River for Ottawa on March 24, 1870, in the company of Colonel Charles de Salaberry, one of the early emissaries sent to Red River by the federal government. Ritchot met up with Alfred Scott near present-day Ste. Agathe, Manitoba. The two delegates reached St. Cloud, Minnesota, by stagecoach on April 6, where they began the journey to Ottawa. The same week, the *Globe* newspaper in Toronto carried a front-page story of the March 4 execution of Thomas Scott. It was an early sign of the political hornet's nest the Red River negotiating team was about to enter. After hearing about the fierce anti-Riel sentiment brewing in Ontario, Ritchot and Alfred Scott decided on a more clandestine route going forward. After leaving St. Cloud, they took a train to Buffalo and met with Gilbert McMicken of the Dominion Police at Ogdensburg, New York, who escorted them safely, again by train, to Ottawa on April 11. Judge John Black took a different route; he travelled through Detroit to Toronto, then to Ottawa. His wife had died several years earlier, and he journeyed to Ottawa with his sister.

Federal officials were concerned about the growing backlash in Ontario against Riel and his supporters. They not only sought the safe passage of the delegates to Ottawa, they also planned to keep the negotiations as low-key as possible, both for safety and political reasons. Ritchot was introduced to Joseph Howe, secretary of state for the provinces, on April 12. "Mr. Howe received me with politeness," Ritchot wrote in a journal he kept during the talks.[1] But no sooner had Ritchot and Scott arrived in Ottawa

1 Ritchot's journal, in *Manitoba: The Birth of a Province*, vol. I, ed. W.L. Morton (Altona: Manitoba Record Society Publications, 1965), 131. The journal, although limited to Ritchot's perspective, is one of the most important historical documents that provides insight into the backroom dealings that led to the passage of the Manitoba Act. It was written in French and has been translated into English.

than rumours began to swirl about their possible arrest. The same day, the *New York Times* reported that "Indignation over the alleged murder of [Thomas] Scott in Red River by the insurgents continues at Toronto, and the arrest of Riel's delegates is anticipated, should they pass through Ontario."[2]

By then, "indignation meetings" were springing up across southern Ontario and in Montreal, with protesters demanding justice for the "murder" of Thomas Scott and the immediate cancellation of meetings between the federal government and the Red River delegates. The public rallies were fuelled in large part by Canadian Loyalist John Christian Schultz and his supporters, several of whom had travelled from Red River to Toronto prior to the arrival of the delegates to stir up anti-Riel sentiment. Newspapers across Ontario carried weeks of inflammatory stories about the "murderer" Riel and the "outrageous crimes" committed by him and his supporters.

The largest indignation meeting was held in Toronto on April 6, attended by an estimated ten thousand people.[3] Schultz and others addressed the crowd at the meeting, drawing cheers and encouraging Ontarians to demand that the federal government call off talks with the delegates. They claimed the negotiations were illegitimate because the delegates did not represent the majority of the people in Red River. It was a false claim. Convention of Forty representatives, who selected the delegates, were elected from all parishes in the settlement. Even Lord Dufferin, Canada's governor general in 1875, who had his doubts about the legitimacy of the provisional government, acknowledged that the delegates had been selected by a duly elected body. "An attempt has been made to show that these delegates really held their appointment from Riel and were to be considered as commissioned by his Government," he wrote in 1874. "This, however, was not so . . . the terms they were instructed to demand were settled before the election of Riel to the so-called Presidency."[4]

---

[2] *New York Times*, Apr. 12, 1870.

[3] *Daily British Whig*, Kingston, Ontario, Apr. 9, 1870.

[4] Correspondence from Lord Dufferin to the Earl of Carnarvon, Britain's secretary of state for the colonies, Dec. 4, 1874, House of Commons sessional papers, 1875, vol. 7, no. 11, 11.

Several "resolutions" were passed at the massive open-air meeting in Toronto, including a demand that the Red River delegates be prohibited from passing through the city, and that they "should meet the fate of [Thomas] Scott" if caught.[5] One public meeting held in St. Mary's, Ontario, included a resolution "that a reward be offered for Riel's head." At a Montreal meeting, there were cries of "string him up" and "hang him," in reference to Riel.[6] Ritchot, Black and Scott were in hostile territory.

Rumours of the delegates' impending arrest proved true: Alfred Scott was apprehended by police on April 12, the same day the delegates arrived, around 10:00 p.m. Ritchot didn't wait for officers to show up at his door—he turned himself in the next day in the presence of several friends and supporters. This was not at all what the delegates had expected when they left Red River. Any diplomatic immunity they thought they would enjoy as official representatives of Rupert's Land appeared to have evaporated the moment they set foot in Ontario, even though they had been invited by the prime minister to engage in bilateral talks.

The warrants for the arrests were authorized by a sympathetic magistrate in Toronto. They were sworn by Hugh Scott, brother of the executed Thomas Scott, with support from members of Canada First, a small but influential group of anti-French and anti-Catholic populists in Ontario of which Schultz was a member. Ritchot and Alfred Scott were twice arrested on charges of complicity for Scott's killing. The second arrest was authorized by an Ottawa magistrate, also sworn by Hugh Scott.

The two delegates' legal troubles didn't last long. After a few days of house arrest and some legal wrangling, the courts declared the warrants invalid and the delegates were free to resume their diplomatic duties. Meanwhile, the third delegate, John Black, who had not participated directly in the resistance,[7] arrived in Ottawa unmolested.

John A. Macdonald had some choppy political waters to navigate.

---

[5] *Daily British Whig*, Apr. 9, 1870.

[6] *Daily British Whig*, Apr. 9, 1870.

[7] The closest that Judge John Black, who was of British descent, came to participating in the Red River Resistance was his role as chairman of the Convention of Forty. He was not a Riel supporter.

Canada First and its supporters proved to be a thorn in his side. On the one hand, he had to be careful not to alienate his Anglo-Canadian constituency in Ontario, from which he drew the bulk of his political support. On the other, he had Quebec supporters to placate, including the francophone wing of his government caucus—represented largely by George-Étienne Cartier—who were supportive of the Métis cause. The resistance had been widely reported in Ontario and Quebec newspapers over the winter, and divisions were forming along linguistic and religious lines: English Protestants in Ontario and French Catholics in Quebec. Macdonald was also under pressure from the British government, which demanded that Canada negotiate a fair deal with the Red River delegation as part of its purchase of Rupert's Land from the Hudson's Bay Company. When Ritchot and Scott were arrested, the British government immediately cabled Ottawa and demanded to know whether the federal government had approved the warrants. Not only did federal officials have nothing to do with the warrants, they provided the delegates with legal representation to defend themselves in court.

Macdonald required the support of the British government for another reason: he needed its military resources. Regardless of how talks with the Red River delegates turned out, Ottawa was already planning to send a military expedition to Red River to establish Canada's sovereignty in the west. The plan had been in the works for months. Macdonald needed a British battalion to lead the campaign, largely because Canada didn't have regular troops in 1870. London agreed to supply the soldiers, but only if the federal government concluded successful negotiations with the delegates. The British government was opposed to Canada assuming control of the Northwest through military force and insisted on a peaceful transfer of power. Ritchot wasn't aware of that quid pro quo. Had he known, it would have given him greater leverage at the bargaining table. Nevertheless, with the British government breathing down his neck and the Quebec wing of his party demanding a fair deal, Macdonald was motivated on several fronts to negotiate in good faith. Ritchot had a political advantage he wasn't fully aware of.

It took two weeks after the arrival of the delegation for talks to begin, a delay that did not please Ritchot. Both Macdonald and George-Étienne Cartier did most of the bargaining for Canada, but it was the latter who emerged as government's chief negotiator. Macdonald was twice absent from talks, once because he was "indisposed," one of his many bouts with the bottle, and again when he became seriously ill. HBC governor Sir Stafford Northcote, who travelled from London, England, to Ottawa to represent the company during the negotiations with the Red River delegates, wrote in his journal that Macdonald was frequently absent from work because of his alcoholism, which some regarded as a "disease," he said. Macdonald "has for several months been practicing total abstinence from wine and has been getting into a very exhausted state," wrote Northcote. He said Macdonald "has had recourse to the bottle again and is not likely to be up to work before Monday."[8] The HBC governor provided rare insight into Macdonald's alcoholism and how it might have played a role in negotiations with the Red River delegates. He wrote that Canada's governor general at the time, Sir John Young, told him people do not attribute Macdonald's drinking "to vice" but to a "physical state of exhaustion which renders him obliged sometimes to have recourse to a stimulant, and which gives the stimulant a very powerful effect. When he once begins to drink he becomes almost mad and there is no restraining him till the fit is over." Macdonald's frequent absences left Cartier to do most of the negotiating. The full impact of Macdonald's absences will never be known. However, Cartier, who was more sympathetic to the French Métis cause, may have been more amenable to Ritchot's demands than the prime minister would have been had he been present at all the meetings.

Ritchot found an ally in Cartier, a Quebec-born politician who himself was involved in a resistance earlier in his life during the rebellion of 1837, where he fought for responsible government. Negotiations took place in Cartier's Ottawa home, away from the prying eyes of newspaper reporters and others. Ritchot first met Cartier at his home, along with Judge Black and Macdonald, during an informal meeting on April 23. It was there that

[8] "The Ottawa Diary of Sir Stafford Northcote," in *Manitoba: The Birth of a Province*, vol. I, ed. W.L. Morton (Altona: Manitoba Record Society Publications, 1965), 67.

the St. Norbert priest and Cartier discovered they had much in common. Both men spoke French and shared similar cultural backgrounds. "We were received with great courtesy," wrote Ritchot of his first visit. "We were given to understand that we should be given a good government."

Still, the two sides were far apart in the early stages of negotiations. Macdonald and Cartier immediately tested the will of their rookie counterparts. They initially refused to recognize the delegates as official representatives of Red River, proposing instead to hold informal discussions. It wasn't until Ritchot told Macdonald and Cartier that he was reaching the end of his patience that they agreed to acknowledge them—in writing—as formal representatives of the Northwest.

Negotiations began in earnest on April 25. Both sides bargained hard. Macdonald proposed that the settlement should enter Canada as a territory, governed by a lieutenant-governor and an appointed council. It would be a temporary measure, to be followed by provincial status and representative government. Ottawa's position was that Red River was not prepared for full provincial status because of its small size and lack of experience with elections and government bureaucracies. Macdonald suggested that a phase-in period would be more suitable. However, Ritchot was adamant that without immediate provincial status and an elected government, the Indigenous inhabitants of Rupert's Land would be crowded out by Anglo-Canadians by the time elections were held a year or more later.

But John Black agreed with Macdonald.[9] It marked the first of several disagreements between Black and Ritchot during talks. Black was often quick to acquiesce to Ottawa's demands. Ritchot, by contrast, continually pushed for more favourable terms. The differences between the two not only made for awkward talks, they undermined the delegates' bargaining power at the negotiating table.

Two months earlier in Red River, the Convention of Forty had voted down Riel's resolution that Manitoba enter Canada as a province. Black had voiced his opposition to Riel's proposal at the time, making a lengthy

[9] It's unclear where Alfred Scott stood on the issue. Ritchot mentioned him only twice in his journal entries.

speech about why he believed the idea was misguided. It was not surprising, then, that he supported the prime minister's position that Manitoba should enter Canada as a territory. What was surprising was that neither Macdonald nor Cartier cited the Convention of Forty's opposition to the proposal to support their own positions, even though transcripts of the convention's deliberations, including the vote that defeated Riel's provincial status motion, were published in Red River's *New Nation* newspaper, which was read as far away as England.

Ritchot refused to yield to Macdonald's demands on territorial status, prompting the prime minister to seek a compromise. Macdonald proposed to shorten the transition period from territory to province from one year to six months, then to two months. Ritchot refused. The prime minister then suggested a hybrid: a half-elected, half-appointed government. Ritchot still would not budge. The St. Norbert priest insisted the settlement have the same provincial rights as all other Canadian provinces. Macdonald would eventually relent; the settlement would enter Canada with full provincial status, governed by an elected legislative assembly and a senate. Ritchot had won round 1.

The new province would also get representation in Parliament—four seats in the House of Commons and two in the Senate. Ritchot demanded, and won, the use of French and English in the provincial legislature and the courts. Denominational schools would also be enshrined in law.

In return, the delegates had to accept some compromises. Ottawa insisted on maintaining control of Crown lands, not only within the province but outside of it too. The boundaries of the new province would also be severely limited. Ottawa wasn't about to hand over the entire land mass of the North-West Territories (which was bigger than either Ontario or Quebec at the time) to twelve thousand people living in Red River and to First Nations living outside that community. The federal government had bigger plans in store, including the construction of a transcontinental railway as part of its vision to settle the west, and access to Crown lands was needed to accomplish that. They also required land for the Hudson's Bay Company, which, under the agreement to sell Rupert's Land to Canada, was entitled to one-twentieth of the land (as well as "reserves" around their existing trading posts). Land was also needed to negotiate treaties with First Nations.

Ritchot got the provincial status he had demanded, but the geographical size of the new province would be small; not much bigger than what was then known as the District of Assiniboia, a sixty-mile radius around Upper Fort Garry. The "postage stamp" province would span about fourteen thousand square miles. Manitoba's boundaries were expanded in 1881 (thanks to persistent lobbying by Manitoba's first Indigenous premier, the English-speaking Métis John Norquay) and grew to its current size in 1912.

During the negotiations, several battles over land rights took place, including how land holdings would be recognized. The federal government agreed that existing property held by settlers would be honoured by Ottawa. That was important to all Red River inhabitants, including to non-Métis settlers. However, the Métis were also concerned about ensuring their land rights were protected into the future. Ritchot proposed land grants for the Métis, which federal negotiators initially opposed. They argued the Métis could not have it both ways; they could not be granted "civilized government" while at the same time receive land grants based on their Indigenous ancestry. The federal government's position revealed a colonial mentality that coloured much of the talks.

At the April 27 meeting, Ritchot argued with Macdonald and Cartier that it would be unjust for the Métis to hand over all public lands to the Crown without receiving something in return. "We cannot yield those rights without compensation," he wrote, insisting the Métis were entitled to some form of land grant. Black once again opposed Ritchot, saying it was "extravagant" for the inhabitants of the Northwest to claim ownership of public lands when the territory, according to Black, now belonged to the Dominion of Canada. Judge Black's support of Ottawa's position put Ritchot in a difficult position. The St. Norbert priest had to negotiate with federal officials with one hand and fend off the judge with the other. "Not only is it not extravagant but just and reasonable" for the Métis to receive a land grant, he argued.

Despite all odds against him, Ritchot eventually won the day on the land grant provision. It would become one of the most significant aspects of the final agreement approved by Parliament. After a lengthy and heated debate, both Macdonald and Cartier agreed in principle to provide the Métis with an allotment of land. Agreeing on the specifics of that provision would be a different matter.

The federal government's opening offer was one hundred thousand acres to be granted to the children of Métis families. "Impossible to accept that," Ritchot wrote. Ottawa upped the offer to two hundred thousand acres, to be divided among the heads of Métis families and held for their children. Black, still siding with the prime minister, found the offer "very reasonable." Ritchot did not. They adjourned for the day.

The following day, April 28, the delegates were presented with a draft bill of the Manitoba Act. Federal bureaucrats had been working on the bill before the delegates arrived in Ottawa. "We began to examine it, but Sir John was indisposed," wrote Ritchot. "We put off the examination until the next day."[10] Ritchot dined at Cartier's house that evening, along with friends from Montreal. It is unknown what was discussed during the social occasion, including whether Cartier and Ritchot spoke about the negotiations or steered clear of them. Either way, the personal relationship that had developed between Ritchot and Cartier likely had some impact on negotiations.

It was back to business the next day, but Macdonald was still indisposed. The land issue remained unresolved. Ritchot suggested a land grant of three million acres for the Métis. Federal officials dismissed that out of hand. Cartier countered with one million acres; not enough, said Ritchot. The matter was again adjourned until the next day. It took several more days of talks, including discussions about how the land grants would be distributed. And then, finally, a deal: 1.4 million acres of land would be granted to the children of Métis families.

How that land would be distributed became the subject of intense debate for years after 1870. Federal officials at first agreed that the land would be distributed by the provincial government. However, they changed their minds during negotiations and made a unilateral amendment to the bill,

[10] Ritchot's journal, *Manitoba: The Birth of a Province.*

giving that control to Parliament instead. Ritchot protested. In response, federal officials assured him the land grants would be administered through a local committee. Like many of its verbal promises, though, the federal government reneged on that commitment. The land distribution issue would be the subject of a landmark Supreme Court of Canada decision 143 years later in favour of the Métis. Without Ritchot's advocacy at the bargaining table, there would have been no land grants at all for the Métis.

Meanwhile, the delegates were poring over the draft of the Manitoba Act. Ritchot went through it line by line over several days, marking it up with proposed changes and question marks. It was brought back to the negotiating table for further revision. On May 2, Macdonald, back at work after several days of absence, introduced the bill in the House of Commons. The prime minister announced that to honour the original inhabitants of the land "it is considered proper that the province which is to be organized shall be called Manitoba." The name, he explained, was a "euphonious" Indigenous word meaning "The God who speaks—the speaking of God."

There is no definitive explanation of the origins of the name *Manitoba*, although it is largely understood to have been derived from Indigenous language. The name, and Parliament's acceptance of it, further underscores the influence Indigenous people had on Manitoba's entry into Canada. The most commonly accepted explanation of the provincial name is that it comes from the Narrows of Lake Manitoba, where the waves that crash against the limestone rock are said to be the voice of Manitou, or the Great Spirit. In Ojibway it is *Manito-bau*. It's also unclear when, during negotiations, the name was proposed to Macdonald and Cartier. A letter dated April 19 from Riel to Ritchot, where the Métis leader suggested *Manitoba* as one of the names that should be chosen, arrived in Ottawa after the Manitoba Act had been introduced in the House of Commons. It appears Ritchot had proposed the name during negotiations. However, it is unclear on whose advice or direction that proposition was made. Whatever the case, it was accepted by Macdonald and Cartier and approved by Parliament.

The introduction of the Manitoba Act in the House of Commons was a historic moment, one Ritchot surely savoured as he witnessed the debate from the public gallery. The fiery, sometimes ugly, banter in the chamber was also sobering for Ritchot, who along with others from Red River became the subject of fierce personal attacks. Not all MPs agreed with the bill or how it was negotiated. Some members were staunchly opposed to the Riel-led resistance and questioned the legitimacy of the delegates sent from Red River. Liberal MP Mackenzie Bowell (Hastings North, Ont.) referred to Ritchot as "that meek and lowly priest . . . who had done more than any other man in the territory to prevent the entrance of the honourable member for North Lanark [William McDougall] into the Red River country."[11]

McDougall, the former lieutenant-governor designate who was refused entry into Red River six months earlier, had returned to Parliament as the MP for North Lanark in Ontario. He was among several MPs critical of the bill and staunchly opposed to the process the federal government had acceded to in drafting it, including negotiating with the delegates. McDougall described those who participated in the Red River Resistance as "the most disreputable inhabitants of the country" who were "collected together by a bar room loafer."[12] It appears he was referring to Riel (though the Métis leader was neither a drinker nor a frequenter of saloons). He also accused Joseph Howe, the secretary of state for the provinces, of siding with the "rebels" by not diffusing the insurgency when he had been in Red River the previous October and by agreeing to negotiate with the delegates sent to Ottawa. "He [Howe] encouraged treason and was now ready, it would seem, to maintain and to sustain rebel authority in that country,"[13] McDougall charged.

Howe returned fire, alleging that McDougall was guilty of "precipitating a crisis" by issuing a false proclamation while in Pembina and by commissioning Colonel Dennis to organize a militia to topple the provisional government. "My honourable friends here know that there was not one of his colleagues but felt that in issuing this proclamation, he had acted in advance of the sovereign, probably with good intentions, but had misconceived his instructions and exceeded his powers, that he was not the lawful

---

11 House of Commons debate, 1st Parliament, 3rd Session, vol. III, May 10, 1870, 1494.

12 House of Commons debate, May 9, 1870, 1455.

13 House of Commons debate, May 3, 1870, 1337.

government of the territory, and had issued a commission to Colonel Dennis, which no man could read then without horror, or can read now without laughing," Howe said.[14]

Howe also mocked McDougall's characterization of Riel as a "bar room loafer." At least the Métis leader had had "sufficient resolution," he said, to capture John Christian Schultz and his supporters "like a coop of chickens" the previous November, referring to the mass arrest at Schultz's home in Winnipeg during the early days of the resistance. "He [Riel] may be a bar-room loafer, but he had brains enough to coop them up in that house and then to drive them to Fort Garry like a flock of sheep,"[15] Howe said, prompting laughter in the chamber. "And murdered one of them," shot back Alexander Mackenzie, the Liberal opposition leader.[16]

Liberal MP E.V. Bodwell (Oxford South, Ont.) accused Howe of not being content opposing Confederation while he was a politician in Nova Scotia; he had to go to Red River and undermine it there too.[17] "The man who could speak in terms of praise of the rebels at Fort Garry, and compare the loyal settlers who were imprisoned there to fowls in a hen coop, was deserving the contempt of the country, and would be properly estimated by the people of Ontario,"[18] said Bodwell. Alexander Mackenzie ridiculed the new province's small size. He said it "seemed ludicrous" to grant a "little municipality" like Red River provincial status and quipped that it reminded him of the story of *Gulliver's Travels*. And so went the partisan sniping that lasted over a week as the Manitoba Act wound its way through Parliament.

When Macdonald explained why the federal government had agreed to a bicameral system for the new province—an elected legislative assembly of

---

14 House of Commons debate, May 9, 1870, 1474.

15 House of Commons debate, May 9, 1870, 1468.

16 Mackenzie, who would become Canada's second prime minster in 1873, was referring to the execution of Thomas Scott, who was part of the group captured at the Schultz house but wasn't executed until after his second capture the following February.

17 There was no evidence Howe encouraged anyone to participate in the resistance while he was in the Red River Settlement in October 1869, nor was there any reason to believe he was aware the resistance was being planned.

18 House of Commons debate, May 9, 1870, 1481.

twenty-four members and an upper chamber of seven appointed members—it drew sneers from the opposition. "With respect to the Legislative body, there was considerable difficulty and long discussion whether it should consist of one chamber or two," said Macdonald. "After mature consideration, it was agreed that there should be two chambers. I see my hon. friend (Hon. Mr. McDougall) laughs, but, being a true liberal, he will not object to the people having a voice in the settlement of their own Constitution and to determine whether they shall have one or two chambers or even three if it suits their purpose to have them."[19]

Meanwhile, there was considerable debate about whether the three delegates from Red River truly represented the people from the settlement. Opposition MPs asked why others, such as John Christian Schultz and the so-called Canadian Loyalists from the colony, were not part of the talks. Government said the delegates had been chosen by the community through a duly elected body. MP Adams Archibald (Colchester, N.S.), who would be appointed Manitoba's first lieutenant-governor several weeks later, reminded the house that the delegates had been invited to Ottawa by the federal government. "These people are in armed insurrection," said Archibald. "We wish to know what the difficulties are, we invite them to send delegates and they send them on our invitation. The question is not whether the conduct of these people has been right or wrong. We want to know what it is they complain of, and they send these men to tell us. They are, therefore, so far representatives, and any insults hurled against them are insults to the people who sent them here."[20]

Opposition members proposed several amendments to the bill, including a failed attempt to remove the land grant provision for Métis families. Cartier defended the 1.4 million acres reserved for the Métis, arguing that it was fair compensation for the territory they were giving up to Canada. "The land question was the most difficult one to decide of any connected with the measure; it was one of the most important connected with the welfare of the Territory," he said. "Although the Dominion government held the control of the lands it was only just to give something in return for

[19] House of Commons debate, May 2, 1870, 1300–01.

[20] House of Commons debate, May 7, 1870, 1428.

them. Thus arose the reserves. Was it not just and liberal to provide for the settlement of those who had done so much for the advancement of the Red River country—the Indian half-breeds?"[21]

Opposition members also tried, but failed, to reduce voter eligibility from twelve months' residency to one month in the new province, arguing new settlers should be allowed to vote in Manitoba's first election, expected later that year. "The requirement of one year's residence would deprive the best settlers of a vote, while leaving it in the hands of the less educated inhabitants,"[22] said William McDougall, whose prejudice against the Métis was on full display.

Cartier, who opposed the amendment, said the proposed change was "calculated to drown out the half-breeds." New settlers, including some from the military expedition the federal government was planning to send to Red River the following month, were expected to arrive in droves once Manitoba officially joined Canada. If they were allowed to vote within a month of residency (males twenty-one and over were eligible to vote; women did not yet have that right in Canada), they might outnumber Métis voters. Cartier said the intention of sending troops to Red River was to re-establish the authority of the Queen, not to wage war or to affect the outcome of future elections. "Unless authority was re-established and troops sent to maintain it, there was a danger of various sections of the people engaging in civil war, whereas if the law courts were to be able to exercise their powers, they must be supported by the force necessary."[23]

Most of the amendments to the Manitoba Act proposed by the opposition were defeated. However, one did succeed. Portage la Prairie, not part of Manitoba in the original bill, was added to the boundaries at second reading after concerns were raised about its exclusion.[24] The small com-

---

21 House of Commons debate, May 9, 1870, 1446.

22 House of Commons debate, May 9, 1870, 1453.

23 House of Commons debate, May 10, 1870, 1507.

24 It appears this amendment was proposed by Schultz and his supporters who had the ear of opposition members in Ottawa when the Manitoba Act was being debated in the House of Commons.

munity, located just west of Winnipeg, was composed largely of English-speaking Canadians at the time and was seen as an integral part of the new province. John A. Macdonald, who was absent from the House of Commons during the last few days of debate owing to illness (it was believed he was suffering from the passing of gallstones),[25] said government believed initially that the people in Portage la Prairie did not wish to be part of the new province. Once it was made clear to government that that was not the case, the boundaries were redrawn to include the community, said Macdonald.[26]

After more than a week of heated debate, the bill was approved by Parliament and given royal assent on May 12. "At midnight it passed third reading," Ritchot wrote on May 10.[27] "Everybody is pleased with the bill, except the Toronto hotheads, such as McDougall . . ."[28] The Manitoba Act was proclaimed into law by cabinet on July 15, marking the day Manitoba officially joined Canada.

Almost immediately after the Manitoba Act became law, there were questions about its legality. The federal government did not have the constitutional authority under the British North America Act of 1867 to add Manitoba as a province. A series of legal debates was sparked that ultimately led the British government to amend the BNA Act the following year. The change retroactively gave Parliament the authority to create new provinces, which effectively added the Manitoba Act to Canada's constitution. As a result, the provisions negotiated by the Red River delegates, including land rights for the Métis, became constitutionally protected, meaning they could not be unilaterally altered by Ottawa.

His mission largely accomplished, Ritchot wired Riel to inform him of

---

[25] The house was informed on May 7, 1870, by MP John Young Bown, who was a physician, that Macdonald was absent and very ill because he "suffered excruciating torture from what we supposed was the passing of a biliary calculas," House of Commons debate, 1412.

[26] House of Commons debate, May 5, 1870.

[27] Ritchot's journal, *Manitoba: The Birth of a Province.*

[28] Ritchot's journal, *Manitoba: The Birth of a Province.*

the developments in Ottawa. Negotiations were completed "satisfactorily" and the Manitoba Act had passed, he wrote.[29] The Red River community got its first look at the legislation on May 27, when it was published in the *New Nation*.

Ritchot won most of the terms the people of Red River had sought. It was an enormous achievement. Even Judge John Black, despite his persistent opposition to Ritchot during negotiations, paid him a compliment when it was over. "He was pleased with me," wrote Ritchot. "Without me, he said, we should not have had the half of what we had."[30]

Still, one nagging issue remained. When negotiations began, Ritchot insisted—on instructions from Riel and the provisional government—that a general amnesty be granted to those who had participated in the resistance. They wanted an assurance in writing that they would not be prosecuted for actions taken during the fall and winter of 1869–70, including the execution of Thomas Scott. It was an assurance the federal government was reluctant to give, and never did grant in writing at the time. (A general amnesty was issued five years later, but with conditions.)

Federal officials claimed they had no authority to issue an amnesty because Canada had had no jurisdiction over Red River during the resistance, and immunity would have to come from Britain. The amnesty issue became a legal quagmire that dragged on for years. It was a major part of a House of Commons select committee inquiry held in 1874 into the "causes of the difficulties in the North-West Territories in 1869–70," and was never satisfactorily resolved. Both Ritchot and Archbishop Taché claimed at different times that they were promised by federal officials that an amnesty would be forthcoming, which the latter denied.

Alfred Scott and John Black left Ottawa after the passage of the Manitoba Act. Ritchot stayed and continued to lobby Cartier for an amnesty agreement. The best he could get was a verbal assurance that one would eventually come from England. It never did, at least not one that would exonerate all those involved in the execution of Thomas Scott. Ritchot, after travelling to Quebec to spend time with family, returned to Ottawa for more

---

[29] Ritchot's journal, *Manitoba: The Birth of a Province.*

[30] Ritchot's journal, *Manitoba: The Birth of a Province.*

meetings around the amnesty issue before returning home. He arrived in Red River via the steamboat the *International* on June 17. The parish priest was welcomed in Winnipeg with a twenty-one-gun salute and greeted personally by Riel. All were anxious for a full briefing of what had transpired over the previous two months.

Ritchot addressed the legislative assembly on June 24. In his speech,[31] he said not all aspects of the settlement's list of rights had been accepted by the federal government and that negotiations had been difficult at times. Federal ministers were initially opposed to the land grant provision for the Métis, he said. It was only after they were faced with an ultimatum that they agreed to it. "Ministers at first fought very hard against us in this matter. They said you are claiming for the half-breeds the rights and liberties of civilized people, while at the same time you want for them certain rights as Indians. We cannot recognize these two claims. We answered, if you do not want to recognize these rights, do not ask us to enter Confederation. We are not bound to enter the Dominion."[32]

Still, Ritchot continued, the people of Red River had secured important rights for themselves and for future generations and were now in a better position to welcome newcomers to their community. The parish priest thanked Macdonald and Cartier for "the liberal bill framed by them, with the assistance of the delegates," and reminded members of the legislative assembly that the Manitoba Act was overwhelmingly approved by a vote of 120 to 11 in the House of Commons. He also talked about the considerable support in eastern Canada for the people of Red River. "One word, as to the people of Canada with whom we came into contact," said Ritchot. "I found them very kind, generous and fair, and that they did not, as a rule, take the same view of matters which some papers had done. They looked at the occurrences of last winter in their proper light; and while censuring where they thought it deserved, they did not blame the people, as they thought they were in peculiar circumstances."[33]

---

[31] Ritchot addressed the assembly in French, which was translated into English by Louis Riel.

[32] *New Nation*, July 1, 1870.

[33] *New Nation*, July 1, 1870.

Just over seven months after armed Métis horsemen blocked the lieutenant-governor designate at the U.S. border and demanded consultations with the Canadian government, the Manitoba Act was approved by the Legislative Assembly of Assiniboia. It was another historic moment. Assembly member Louis Schmidt introduced the motion, which was carried amid cheers in the chamber. "I would move that the Legislative Assembly of this country do now, in the name of the people, accept the Manitoba Act, and decide on entering the Dominion of Canada, on the terms proposed in the Confederation Act."[34] Local merchant Alexander Begg marked the day in his journal as "the turning point in the affairs of the Settlement,"[35] celebrated that night with drink and merriment by members of the legislative assembly.

In their struggle for self-determination, Riel and his provisional government had not gotten everything they wanted from Ottawa. The question of amnesty would hang in the balance. Years of delay and bureaucratic bungling by the federal government on the 1.4-million-acre land distribution issue proved damaging to the Métis community. As predicted, Canadians flooded the new province almost immediately after Manitoba entered Confederation and snapped up valuable property. Many Métis families moved west. To some extent, their worst fears came true—that by joining Canada, their way of life would be dramatically altered.

Still, the decision to take up arms to protect their democratic, linguistic and land rights had yielded some tangible benefits. It was by no means a fruitless effort. As inadequate and inequitable as the process had been, land, and later scrip in lieu of land, was distributed to Métis families. The land and language rights the Métis won were subsequently upheld by the Supreme Court of Canada. In many ways, the actions of the Métis were vindicated.

---

[34] *New Nation,* July 1, 1870.

[35] Alexander Begg, entry for June 24, 1870, in *Alexander Begg's Red River Journal and Other Papers Relative to the Red River Resistance of 1869–70,* edited by W.L. Morton, 384. Toronto: The Champlain Society, 1956.

CHAPTER 5

...

Waiting for Canada

IF THE MÉTIS HAD any second thoughts about their decision in October to block a federally appointed lieutenant-governor from entering their settlement, a speech by the would-be Queen's representative eight months later probably put those doubts to rest. William McDougall, the MP for North Lanark, Ontario, chosen by prime minister John A. Macdonald as Manitoba's first lieutenant-governor in 1869, but prevented from entering the Red River Settlement, returned to Ottawa later that year. Following his return to Parliament as an MP, he complained in a vile, bigoted speech to his constituents that all the valuable land in Manitoba had been taken up by the Métis:

> The only land, indeed, that any intelligent Canadian would seek, in the early settlement of the country to purchase or to cultivate, is "reserved," locked up in the hands of lazy and ignorant half-breeds, without any claim whatever to this larger part of it, and for no purpose that anyone can see but to keep out white men, or to put money into

> the pockets of the priests. This reserved tract contains the water and timber, and the river system, which constitutes the highway of the emigrant and trader. It contains all that is at present of any value to the province.[1]

This and other excerpts of McDougall's speech were published in Manitoba's only newspaper at the time, the *New Nation*. The paper's editor said it ran the excerpts as proof that the decision to block McDougall from entering the community was the right one. "His delicate reference to our 'lazy, ignorant half-breeds,' is very flattering to our industrious and enterprising native farmers, the results of whose long labour and toil may now be seen on the banks of the Red River and Assiniboine, where some farms may be found to equal, if not exceed, in extent of cultivation and general prosperity, anything that Mr. McDougall can show among his favourites of North Lanark," the newspaper wrote. Surely the most deserving people to occupy the "good" land were those who were born and raised in Red River, the newspaper added. That, along with the protection of language and democratic rights, was the whole point of the resistance. "[McDougall's] language is that of the ruined and desperate politician and agitator, certainly not the statesman he was supposed to be at one time," the newspaper wrote. "And it is well for the people of this country that Providence ordained he should never rule over them." If the strong majority vote in Parliament in favour of the Manitoba Act was any indication, McDougall's venomous remarks were not shared by a majority of Canadians at the time. Nevertheless, racism and colonial mentalities were alive and well in 1870 Canada, as evidenced by the large rallies in Ontario that spring opposing the Métis-led provisional government.

That summer, as the people of Red River awaited the arrival of the new lieutenant-governor, Adams Archibald, as well as the military expedition on its way from Ottawa, some couldn't help but feel a sense of trepidation. Would there be a peaceable transition of power? Would the federal government honour the property rights, land grants and other provisions

---

1 *New Nation*, July 23, 1870.

contained in the Manitoba Act? Would Manitobans encounter bigoted, hateful views—like those of McDougall and John Christian Schultz—from new settlers?

Manitobans were busy in the summer of 1870, farming and getting furs to market. More than one hundred carts of buffalo robes, otter, mink, lynx, beaver and other furs from Winnipeg merchants Bannatyne & Begg were already on their way to St. Cloud, Minnesota, for shipment to various parts of the world. Two hundred more carts were expected to get to market that year. There was a sense by many that joining Canada would take the settlement to new economic heights. A road from Lake of the Woods, Ontario, was nearing completion, and the idea of a railroad from the east to Winnipeg was no longer a pipe dream. Regular mail would soon come to Winnipeg with three deliveries a week. Same-day telegraph service was less than a year away. Red River was about to graduate from a small frontier town with limited trading opportunities to a rapidly growing province with access to broader markets in the east. "We are glad to know that amongst their shipments there is a large one to Canada," the *New Nation* wrote of the Bannatyne & Begg exports. "This is as it should be, for when we are united to the Dominion, trade will be the strongest tie to bind us together . . . Let Canada prove itself a good market for our exports, and she will derive thousands—we may say millions—of dollars from this country. We, on the other hand, will be large consumers of such articles as the merchants of the Dominion are in a position to furnish us."[2]

Not everyone in eastern Canada saw the benefits of annexation, however. Some in Ontario were concerned that the financial costs of inviting Manitoba into the constitutional fold would be a drain on the federal treasury. The *Hamilton Weekly Times* wondered when the rest of Canada would benefit financially from the expansion, given the steep cost of buying Rupert's Land from the Hudson's Bay Company (paid for through a loan from the British government) and the ongoing federal subsidies required to pay for government administration, infrastructure and transportation in Manitoba. "What are we to get in return for all this large expenditure?" the

2 *New Nation*, July 16, 1870.

newspaper asked in a July 14 editorial. "We shall have a vastly extended territory without doubt. The Dominion will embrace an area larger than that of the whole United States. But that will not necessarily bring in any return for the large amount of capital we shall be called upon to expend in various ways, upon our new purchase."[3]

Meanwhile, the *New Nation* was remarkably complimentary of John A. Macdonald, especially for a newspaper that served as an organ for Métis leader Louis Riel's provisional government. Despite the prime minister's attempt the previous year to unilaterally annex Red River without consulting its inhabitants, the newspaper praised him for ultimately doing the right thing by negotiating Manitoba's terms of entry into Canada. "As soon as he discovered the blunders into which his government had been led, regarding this country, he at once took steps to repair them in a statesman-like fashion,"[4] the newspaper wrote.

In hindsight, the federal government recognized it had erred in its attempt to annex Rupert's Land without consulting the people who lived there. Many of the "troubles" in Red River could have been avoided had federal officials taken steps to communicate with the people living in the settlement prior to the transfer, according to a brief prepared by the federal government in 1874 for the House of Commons Select Committee on the Causes of the Difficulties in the North-West Territory in 1869–70. Federal officials even appeared to accept some responsibility for the uprising. They also didn't mince words when it came to McDougall's role in it.

> The troubles in the North-West broke out unexpectedly. They are mainly attributable to the hasty and inconsiderate manner in which surveys were entered upon by Dominion officials, of lands which the half-breeds considered theirs; to the fact that a transfer was made by the Hudson [*sic*] Bay Company, and a Lieutenant-Governor appointed, without any notice to or consideration for the people of the territory. The opposition, which might easily have been satisfied by slight guarantee, became intensified by the haughty conduct of

---

[3] Reprinted in the *New Nation*, Aug. 6, 1870.

[4] *New Nation*, July 16, 1870.

> Mr. McDougall, which brought about an open and armed resistance to the Dominion authorities.[5]

Donald A. Smith, who returned to Manitoba in the summer of 1870 and won a seat in Manitoba's first legislative assembly in December, said there was plenty of blame to go around when assessing the events that led to the Red River Resistance, including from outside the settlement. During debate in the legislative assembly in 1872 Smith said an investigation into the uprising would show that the actions of "outsiders" were a major cause. "Such an investigation, from the commencement of the troubles of 1869, would show that faults lay, not with one side, but with many," said Smith, adding that actors "outside this country and Ontario" were "not entirely blameless in this matter."[6]

Even *The Manitoban* newspaper,[7] which was not a supporter of Louis Riel and the provisional government, wrote in an editorial in 1871 that the uprising was not a "rebellion." Rather, it was a reaction to Canada's attempt to assume control of the Red River Settlement without the input of the people. "Riel himself, it is well known, never pronounced against British supremacy: he always hoisted the British flag, but objected to Canada taking possession of this country, without giving its people the right to pronounce on the intended absorption." The newspaper said it was wrong for Riel and his men to "plunder" the HBC and to execute Thomas Scott. But the assertions from those in eastern Canada that the resistance was the handiwork of "rebels" was inaccurate. "It may have been very annoying to have their representative, the Hon. Wm. McDougall, sent back from the frontier; but that was not rebellion, for at that time Canada had no legal status in this country."[8]

On some fronts, life was returning to normal in Red River after a bitter

---

[5] Memorandum on *Report of the Select Committee*, House of Commons sessional papers, 1875, vol. 7, no. 11, 19.

[6] Manitoba legislative assembly debates, Feb. 2, 1872, in *The Manitoban*, Feb. 5, 1872.

[7] *The Manitoban* began publication in October 1870 after the *New Nation* was shut down by anti-Riel actors following the arrival of Wolseley's troops in August 1870.

[8] *The Manitoban*, Apr. 15, 1871.

resistance that pitted settler against settler. Some of those wounds left lasting scars that took years to heal. Nevertheless, by the summer of 1870, the constant fear of violent outbreaks and arbitrary detention while under martial law was subsiding. The people of Red River could take a breath, at least temporarily. On July 15, they officially became Manitobans and Canadians. For many, there was hope that the quality of their lives would improve as new citizens of the fledgling Dominion. For others, particularly some Métis, the trust and faith they had put into joining the federation would soon be put to the test.

CHAPTER 6

...

The Wolseley Expedition

JOHN A. MACDONALD had begun making plans to send a military force to Red River months before the Manitoba Act was approved by Parliament. The prime minister didn't publicize it at the time, but preliminary discussions to send troops to the Northwest to establish Canadian sovereignty started as early as December 1869. Macdonald wrote on December 16—more than two months before the execution of Thomas Scott—that he hoped the emissaries the federal government sent to Red River, including Donald A. Smith, would succeed in restoring order in the colony. Failing that, however, "the government are making preparations, by the construction of boats, and otherwise, for sending a military force in early spring," the prime minister wrote.[1]

Officially, it would be a mission of peace to help manage the settlement and "cause law and order to be respected," Macdonald told the House of Commons almost five months later (the same day he unveiled details of the

[1] John A. Macdonald, copy of a report by a committee of the privy council, Dec. 16, 1869, House of Commons sessional papers, 1870, vol. 5, no. 12, 144.

proposed Manitoba Act). He assured Parliament the expedition would be deployed "in no hostile spirit." But that was not how it played out on the ground.

The Red River Expedition, as it was named, was a well-armed, battle-ready force made up of British soldiers and a volunteer Canadian militia, many of whom had vengeance on their minds and a thirst to topple the "rebellion" at Red River. Colonel Garnet Wolseley, a career British soldier experienced in combat operations around the world, was chosen as field commander. He headed the 60th Rifles, a force of 373 officers and men who represented the core of the expedition. This would be the British military's final operation in North America. In addition to regular British troops, Wolseley had command of two militia battalions, one from Ontario and one from Quebec, though most of those from the Quebec contingent were Ontarians. Many who signed up as volunteers were eager to avenge the death of Thomas Scott. In total, the expedition numbered more than twelve hundred.

The quickest and easiest way to travel between eastern Canada and Red River in 1870 was by train through the United States. However, there was no chance that American authorities would allow British and Canadian troops to pass through their territory. That left the expedition with no choice but to use the old voyageur route through the Great Lakes and overland. The ink was barely dry on the Manitoba Act when Wolseley left Collingwood, Ontario, on May 21, 1870, with the first detachment of fifty-one men. They travelled by steamship through Lake Huron and Lake Superior. The soldiers carried Snider breech-loading rifles with sixty rounds of ammunition. Some also brought their own revolvers. The remaining detachments followed in subsequent days. All battalions reached Thunder Bay by June 13. It was an arduous three-month journey through rough terrain, often in gruelling, mosquito-infested conditions. The men endured long portages and braved rough rapids. Wolseley arrived at Fort Frances on July 31. By then, word had arrived in Red River that the military expedition was nearing.

Wolseley informed Manitobans that the expedition was a mission of peace. He had sent a proclamation to the settlement several weeks earlier, which Riel published in the *New Nation* newspaper. The document made no mention of prosecuting those who participated in the resistance, only that "justice will be impartially administered to all races and to all classes." "The sole object of the expedition is to secure Her Majesty's sovereign authority," it read. "The force which I have the honor of commanding will enter your province representing no party either in religion or politics, and will afford equal protection to the lives and property of all races and of all creeds."[2]

The troops, in fact, were spoiling for a fight and had every intention of capturing Riel and the "murderers" of Scott. The official intention of the expedition may have been one of peace and diplomacy, but on the ground, soldiers were eager to do battle. Wolseley made that clear in various subsequent writings. "We had looked forward to advancing on the Fort in all the pride, pomp, and circumstance of war."[3]

The expedition made its way along the Winnipeg River and arrived at Fort Alexander on August 20. The militia was close behind. By the summer of 1870, Riel no longer had the military force he had commanded over the winter months as many Métis were off on the buffalo hunt. Riel could not have mounted much of an armed resistance even if he had wanted to. Aside from that, after the Manitoba Act was approved by Parliament in May, the provisional government was under the impression there would be a peaceful transition of power. Nobody in Red River, including Riel, was expecting a fight; there was no reason to. By then, most were looking forward to the end of what had been a long and disruptive period in their lives.

The federal government had originally planned to send Manitoba's newly appointed lieutenant-governor, Adams Archibald, to Red River prior to the arrival of the troops. Under that scenario, a peaceful transition of power between the Legislative Assembly of Assiniboia and the new Queen's representative could have taken place. However, Archibald did not reach Red River until nine days after Wolseley's arrival, a logistical

---

[2] *New Nation*, July 23, 1870.

[3] A narrative written by Wolseley and printed in *Blackwood's Edinburgh Magazine*, January–June, 1871, 176.

mix-up—or perhaps an intended outcome—that was never clearly explained by officials in Ottawa. Rather than travelling through the U.S. by train to Manitoba as William McDougall had done less than a year earlier, Archibald took the long route through Canada and trailed most of the troops by at least a week. As a result, the transfer of power occurred at the end of a bayonet instead of through a more peaceful and formal process.

On August 21, Wolseley and eight brigades of British soldiers in fifty boats camped at Elk Island just north of Victoria Beach on Lake Winnipeg. The next day, they made their way to the mouth of the Red River and rowed upstream to Lower Fort Garry, north of Winnipeg. They were greeted with cheers from mostly English-speaking settlers, who waved handkerchiefs and rang church bells from the banks of the Red River. Following a planned meal at the Stone Fort, they stayed the night under heavy rainfall. Wolseley sent two spies into Winnipeg ahead of the arrival of the troops to "gain information" about the status of Riel and his men.[4] According to Wolseley, they were told Riel was still in the fort and was prepared to fight. The intelligence he received was false. There were no plans to resist the expedition; few Métis were left at Upper Fort Garry.

It was obvious by then to Riel and the provisional government that there would be no peaceful transition of power. Bishop Alexandre-Antonin Taché of St. Boniface, who had been away in Rome for much of the Red River Resistance, told Riel he had been assured by the federal government that Archibald would arrive before the troops. Taché had travelled to Ottawa a month earlier in a failed attempt to secure an amnesty for Riel and others. By late August, Archibald had still not arrived. Taché had been deceived.

On the morning of August 24, Riel got word that the troops were just a few miles downriver. The Métis leader, realizing he had been misled, bolted from the south gate of Upper Fort Garry mid-breakfast. He crossed the river to St. Boniface and cut the ferry cable behind him. He called on Taché and invited him to witness the arrival of the British military with his own eyes. They watched from across the Red River as the troops docked their

---

[4] Wolseley's narrative, 175–176.

boats and headed towards the empty fort. It was raining heavily and the troops marched through deep mud with guns at the ready. "Notwithstanding all these drawbacks, the men's pace was most elastic, and they were in the highest spirits at the prospect of a fight,"[5] wrote Wolseley.

The troops entered the fort through the south doors, which had been left open by Riel. Finding no one inside, they ransacked parts of it, looking for whatever documentation and evidence they could find. "[Not finding Riel] was at first a sad disappointment to the soldiers, who, having gone through so much toil in order to put down the rebellion, longed to be avenged upon its authors,"[6] wrote Wolseley. By that point, Riel realized there was no chance that Wolseley and his troops would honour the federal government's commitment of a peaceful transition of power. Knowing his safety was in jeopardy, he headed south. "I knew he [Wolseley] would murder me if he caught me, and I always kept ahead of him," Riel said in an interview thirteen years later.[7] "While Wolseley was in the fort, I was talking to Archbishop Taché at his place on the other side of the river. While he [Wolseley] was speaking to his soldiers in front of the fort, I passed by on horseback, along the road, very quietly. I heard them calling the half-breeds bandits."

Archibald wouldn't arrive for another nine days. In his absence, Wolseley put HBC executive Donald A. Smith, who had returned to the settlement, in charge of the new province until the lieutenant-governor's arrival. With the Legislative Assembly of Assiniboia dissolved, and owing to the hostile presence of the military expedition, Smith reconstituted the former Council of Assiniboia, the appointed governing body that had existed prior to the resistance. It was this body, in the presence of Wolseley, that officially received Archibald during a levee (an official ceremony welcoming Archibald as Manitoba's lieutenant-governor) held September 6, at which time his commission was formally read.[8] It was as if the Legislative Assembly of

---

[5] Wolseley's narrative, 177.

[6] Wolseley's narrative, 177.

[7] *Winnipeg Daily Sun*, June 29, 1883.

[8] Archibald had already been officially sworn in as lieutenant-governor in July by Governor General John Young.

Assiniboia—the second provisional government established by the Métis—had never existed.

The Canadian militia remained in the settlement after the departure of Wolseley and the British troops.[9] They were tasked with keeping the peace, although many of the soldiers did the opposite. Some of them exacted the revenge they were looking for. There were brawls in saloons between Canadian soldiers and Métis residents and reports of physical and verbal abuse against local settlers. Elzéar Goulet, one of Riel's supporters and a member of the military tribunal that sentenced Thomas Scott to death, was murdered. Goulet, a French Métis who had become an American citizen while working as a mail carrier between Pembina and Winnipeg, was chased to the Red River by an angry mob that included Canadian soldiers. He drowned after being struck in the head with a stone. Goulet's death was investigated, but no one was ever prosecuted or held responsible for the killing.

It wasn't long before the Canadian Loyalists in Red River who opposed the Métis—many of whom had been jailed and then exiled from the settlement by the provisional government during the resistance, including John Schultz—would get the revenge they had long sought. Four days after Archibald's arrival, Schultz and a mob of his supporters broke into the home of Thomas Spence, the publisher of the *New Nation*, tore him from his bed, horsewhipped him in front of his terrified wife and sabotaged the paper's printing press. It was the beginning of what became known as "the reign of terror" in the new province after the arrival of military troops. Whatever goodwill had grown out of talks between Red River delegates and the federal government earlier that year had vanished.

Schultz, who administered the beating on Spence, was back in Red River after stirring up anti-Métis sentiment in Ontario during the spring and summer. He and his "Canada First" supporters were now focused on seeking retribution against anyone who had taken part in the Red River Resistance. Their goal was to rid the settlement of as many Métis as possible

---

9 All the British troops left Red River by September 3. Wolseley departed Red River for Ottawa on September 10.

to clear the way for new settlers from Ontario. A year after his arrival, in October 1871, Archibald described to the prime minister in stark terms the racism that existed in Manitoba: "Unfortunately there is a frightful spirit of bigotry among a small but noisy section of our people. The main body of the people have no such feeling—they would be only too happy to return to the original state of good neighbourhood with each other; but it is otherwise with the people I speak of, who really talk and seem to feel as if the French half-breeds should be wiped off the face of the globe."[10] Archibald said the Métis had been so badly "beaten and outraged" that they felt as if "they were living in a state of slavery."

Wolseley helped fuel those hostilities. He wrote several times about his desire to capture and punish Métis leader Louis Riel, even though the military expedition was supposed to have been one of peace. The commander said he was disappointed that the Métis didn't resist his troops because it deprived his men of a good battle. Even though George-Étienne Cartier—the federal government's key cabinet negotiator—called on the Legislative Assembly of Assiniboia to govern the settlement until the arrival of the new lieutenant-governor, Wolseley treated the provisional legislative assembly as an enemy of the state.

Wolseley revealed years later in his memoirs how he truly felt about the military expedition, the resistance and the people of Red River. In his book, *The Story of a Soldier's Life*, Wolseley did not hide his disdain for the French, the Métis and especially Riel. "Personally, I was glad that Riel did not come out and surrender, as he at one time said he would, for I could not then have hanged him as I might have done had I taken him prisoner when in arms against his sovereign,"[11] he wrote. Wolseley made scornful references to the "half-breed enemy," the "ridiculous little republic the French party had set up at Fort Garry" and how the whole "rebellion" was fomented by

---

[10] Letter from Adams Archibald to Prime Minister John A. Macdonald, Oct. 9, 1871, in the *Report of the Select Committee on the Causes of the Difficulties in the North-West Territory 1869–70*, (Ottawa: I.B. Taylor, 1874), 157.

[11] Garnet Joseph Wolseley, *The Story of a Soldier's Life*, vol. II (New York: Charles Scribner's Sons, 1903), 220.

Catholic priests. He confirmed that the troops he had led had every intention of fighting the Métis and looked forward to a good battle. According to Wolseley's account, this was not a mission of peace, as the federal government and Wolseley himself, through the proclamation he sent to Red River, had claimed at the time.

"Most of us felt we had to settle accounts quickly with Riel, who had murdered the Englishman, Mr. Scott," Wolseley wrote. "Had we caught him he would have had no mercy."[12] Wolseley characterized the Red River Resistance as an attempt by the "ignorant French 'habitant,'" in response to the growing domination of English settlers in Ontario, to establish a French-speaking country west of the Great Lakes that would act as a "counterpoise" to British Ontario. "All this plot, however, fell to pieces, like a castle of cards, the day I hoisted the Union Jack over Fort Garry."[13]

Wolseley described Riel as a murderer who had manipulated the people of Red River and convinced them to rebel against Canada. "The foremost man amongst these noisy idlers was Louis Riel, a pure French Canadian, though generally referred to as a half-breed. He had, however, many half-breed relations, and wished for political purposes to be considered one himself."[14] Riel spoke well and fluently, and Wolseley wrote that Riel "conceived the idea that in the ignorant community of Red River half-breeds, his superior ability and education ought to secure him an easy mode of livelihood."[15] After the execution of Thomas Scott, the federal government had no choice but to deploy troops to Red River to topple the "rebellion," wrote Wolseley. "The English-speaking people of Canada were so determined to have it put down, that had the government refused to comply, the men of Ontario would have taken the matter into their own hands and have settled it themselves."[16]

Wolseley detailed the excitement and anticipation of war once the troops docked their boats along the muddy banks of the Red River and

---

12 Wolseley, *A Soldier's Life*, 178.

13 Wolseley, 168.

14 Wolseley, 169.

15 Wolseley, 170.

16 Wolseley, 173.

approached Fort Garry. "I confess that I hoped each moment to see a flash and to hear a round shot rush by me."[17] Once it became clear there would be no battle, the troops were deflated, especially after such a long and arduous journey, wrote Wolseley. They had not only hoped for a bloody encounter, they had anticipated one and were prepared to take justice into their own hands if they apprehended Riel. "It was a galling disappointment, for all the ranks were keenly anxious to pitch into those cruel half-breed rebels and longed to hang Riel on the spot where he had murdered the unoffending Mr. Scott."[18]

Wolseley left no doubt about the true intention of the military expedition, at least from his perspective as field commander. If the operation were truly designed at the political level as a mission of peace, as Macdonald and his cabinet had assured Canadians, there was a shocking disconnect between the political and military arms of government in how that mission was deployed.

---

17 Wolseley, 219.

18 Wolseley, 209.

CHAPTER 7

. . .

The Reign of Terror

ADAMS ARCHIBALD, a Nova Scotian and a Father of Confederation, had a daunting task ahead of him. He had the unenviable responsibility of trying to calm the hostilities between the pro-Riel and anti-Métis forces while building a new government with an elected legislative assembly and an appointed senate. He needed a police force, new laws and the co-operation of all segments of the population to make it work. Archibald was somewhat sympathetic to the plight of the Métis, which helped him build goodwill in the settlement, but it was a position he would later be criticized for by political pundits in Ontario. It may have been one of the reasons he was replaced as lieutenant-governor after only two years on the job.

Archibald had a remarkably good read on the complexities of Red River and understood the competing forces within the settlement. But he also failed to crack down on the persistent attacks against the Métis, including by members of the Canadian militia who were left behind by Wolseley. A proclamation issued in September 1870 by Alfred Boyd, who was appointed provincial secretary by Archibald, forbidding people to "take the law into his or their own hands" appeared to have little effect. Within two weeks of his arrival, Archibald had a clear picture of the divisions that existed within the settlement. "There is a very great uneasiness among the population. The French assert that they were promised an amnesty, and many of them declare there can be no solid peace till that promise is fulfilled. The English party, many of whom were sufferers in the late troubles, declare that it is impossible peace can prevail, till the principal actors in the late troubles are arrested and punished, and they are very uneasy lest it should be the intention of government to pass over all these matters and let the men from whom they have suffered go unpunished."[1]

One of the reasons the new government had trouble keeping the peace in Red River was that it had no police force. While the volunteer militia left behind by Wolseley was tasked with securing Canadian sovereignty and maintaining peace in the early days, the new government was loath to use it for law enforcement after Archibald took office. "The soldiers who are here were never intended to act as policemen," wrote Boyd. "No free country asks or suffers soldiers to perform police duties. When the civil authorities are resisted, then the soldiers may be called in to aid, but it is only on such emergencies they can be used."[2]

One problem was that few, if any, of the local settlers were willing to sign up to become police officers. When government officials advertised the positions—at a pay rate higher than in other provinces—no one applied. It appeared no one was prepared to take on the role of police officer in such a hostile environment. "Without some such force, it is absolutely impossible to carry on civil government in the country, or provide for emergencies of the present," wrote Boyd in response to a petition received by government to arrest and prosecute the leaders of the resistance. "Not a man of those who have signed the petitions has offered himself in terms of the appeal to take his share in the indispensable work of protecting the public peace."[3] The provincial government would eventually invite members of

---

1 Letter from Adams Archibald to Joseph Howe, Sept. 17, 1870, House of Commons sessional papers, 1871, vol. 5, no. 20, 16.

2 Attached to letter from Adams Archibald to Joseph Howe, Oct. 8, 1870, House of Commons sessional papers, 1871, vol. 5, no. 20, 49.

3 Archibald to Howe, Oct. 8, 1870, 49.

the Canadian militia to apply for the police positions. Many did and were subsequently hired.

John Christian Schultz was the chief antagonist in Red River in 1870. After shutting down the *New Nation* newspaper and attacking its publisher, Schultz launched his own publication called the *Manitoba News-Letter*. He used it as an attempt to control the political message in the new province. The monopoly didn't last long. Long-time journalist William Coldwell co-founded *The Manitoban* the following month, October, using the restored *New Nation* printing presses. It marked the beginning of a bitter newspaper feud that lasted well into the following year. Very little of the violence against the Métis was reported in either local newspaper—the *News-Letter*, for obvious reasons, and *The Manitoban*, for less obvious ones. However, many newspapers outside the province, including from Minnesota, Quebec and Ontario, carried reports of the so-called reign of terror, a period that left a black mark on the early days of Manitoba.

Several publications sent correspondents to the settlement to report on the activities in Canada's newest province, including the St. Paul *Daily Press* from Minnesota. "During the fall and early winter of 1870 we could always rely on several exciting fights between the soldiers and half breeds any afternoon after three o'clock, by which hour the soldiers who were not on duty at the garrison were at liberty to come downtown," the newspaper wrote in March 1871.[4]

The list of reported attacks against Métis residents after the arrival of Wolseley's troops is long. André Nault, who played a significant role in the resistance, was chased and beaten nearly to death in Pembina by Canadian militia soldiers in March 1871. In December 1870 James Tanner, a prominent English Métis, suffered a fractured skull after two unknown assailants startled his horse, causing him to be thrown from his buggy. He died of his injuries. James Ross, one of the key leaders among the English Métis during the resistance, had his unoccupied two-storey house in Winnipeg torched by unknown arsonists. Witnesses saw the fire start at both ends of the house. The Quebec newspaper *La Minerve* reported that Métis Louis

[4] St. Paul *Daily Press*, Mar. 15, 1871.

Hibbert from the Qu'Appelle Lakes, who came to Manitoba, was assaulted by soldiers and beaten with belts. He might have been killed if two women had not intervened.

The accusations prompted Colonel Garnet Wolseley to defend the reputation of the Canadian troops. During a speech he delivered at a dinner held in his honour in Montreal on September 29, 1870, the British commander said the soldiers were as well behaved as could be expected under the circumstances. "The evil reports spread in the newspapers as to the lawlessness and disorder said to be existing at Fort Garry are greatly exaggerated and highly coloured," he said. "In a country where deeds of violence had so recently been perpetrated, it cannot be expected that everything will be forgotten in a day by those who have suffered from them."[5]

Reports of lawlessness in Red River were not limited to newspaper reports. Archibald confirmed on several occasions the ongoing violence in Red River, even more than a year after he took office. In December 1871, a group of armed Canadian militia volunteers barged into the home of Louis Riel's mother (Julie Lagimodière Riel), looking for the Métis leader—who was still in hiding—and threatening his family. Archibald provided testimony of the home invasion at an 1874 House of Commons select committee hearing on the causes of the resistance: "A party of some eight or ten disbanded volunteers[6] had, without warrant, made a raid on the house of Riel's mother, with faces masked and armed with revolvers, when they committed outrages that had excited the French half-breeds almost to a frenzy."[7]

Archibald described the violence against the Métis in broader terms in a November 1871 memorandum. The report provided further evidence that one of the reasons many Canadians enlisted in Wolseley's expedition was to avenge the death of Thomas Scott. "Some of them openly stated that they had taken a vow before leaving home to pay off all scores by shooting down any Frenchman that was in any way connected with that event," Archibald wrote. "The great bulk of the French population having been, one way or

---

[5] *The Manitoban*, Oct. 22, 1870.

[6] Former members of the Canadian militia.

[7] Archibald testimony, in *Report of the Select Committee on the Causes of the Difficulties in the North-West Territory 1869–70*, (Ottawa: I.B. Taylor, 1874), 162.

other, concerned in the troubles, the feeling gradually grew to be one of intense dislike towards the whole race, which was heartily reciprocated by the French."[8] Time did not heal those wounds, at least not in the short term. According to Archibald, the situation became worse. "When the volunteers came to be disbanded, and were thus freed from all restraint, the hatred of the two classes exhibited itself more and more. Some of the immigrants from Ontario shared the feelings of the disbanded volunteers, and acted in concert with them."[9]

Even *The Manitoban*, which reported very little of the attacks against the Métis after Wolseley's arrival, grew frustrated with the violence and blamed Schultz and his supporters for the unrest. "Can anything more scandalous be conceived than this constant and persistent inciting to violence and mob law?" the newspaper wrote.[10] Newspapers in the United States took note of the violence in Red River. The *New York Tribune* and the *Philadelphia Evening Bulletin* both published the following story on October 5, 1870, under the headline "Outrages at Red River: An American citizen murdered—other outrages committed by the new party in power." The story described the violence as a "reign of terror":

> The Red River Correspondent of The St. Paul *Daily Press* sends that paper an account of what appears to have been the wanton murder, by the Canadians and partisans of Schultz at Winnipeg, of Isidore Goulet [*sic*].[11] It seems he was pointed out as a sympathizer with Riel, was chased, beaten and driven into the Red River, where, while trying to swim away from his pursuers, he was assaulted with stones, and his blood-thirsty assassins were not satisfied until their victim had sunk. The same correspondence contains an account of the horsewhipping of Mr. Spence, the editor of the *New Nation*, by Dr. Schultz, and of the attempt to murder a Catholic priest by Orangemen.

---

8 Archibald memorandum, in *Report of the Select Committee*, 140.

9 Archibald memorandum, 140.

10 *The Manitoban*, Dec. 10, 1870.

11 His name was Elzéar Goulet.

> These high-handed outrages were but the initial proceedings of a reign of terror inaugurated by Dr. Schultz and his partisans, having for its purpose the somewhat comprehensive programme of driving out by threats or actual violence all the French half-breed population, all American citizens, the Hudson's Bay Company, and Gov. Archibald, who, having been appointed under Lower Canadian influences, they do not regard as favoring their schemes of violence.
>
> Isidore Goulet [*sic*] was an American citizen. The American Vice-Consul at Winnipeg, Mr. Robinson, therefore, took prompt measures to recover the body of the murdered man and to have him decently interred, and sent his property to Pembina for safe-keeping. But in doing this he incurred the wrathful indignation of the Schultz party and the Canadian volunteers, who have threatened to shoot, hang, and otherwise maltreat the Vice-Consul.
>
> So thorough is the reign of terror which has been established by the Schultz party, backed by the Canadian volunteers, that no witness dare testify to the facts in the case of the murder of Goulet. But the proceedings which caused his death and the wounds he received were seen by witnesses who can tell on American soil what it would cost them their lives to utter at Winnipeg, and that evidence will in due time be taken and forwarded to the United States Government. That the Canadian volunteers participated in this assassination of an American citizen is evident from the fact that their commanding officer made it the subject of a severe censure and the occasion of an order prohibiting the volunteers from going to the town of Winnipeg, or of mingling in any manner with political gatherings or demonstrations. A Vigilance Committee has been formed under the auspices of Dr. Schultz for the purpose of carrying out his programme of violence and terrorism, and among other patriotic objects, he proposes to drive out all American citizens from Winnipeg and thereabouts.[12]

The refusal by local authorities to prosecute those responsible for the death of Elzéar Goulet left a deep wound in the French Métis community.

---

[12] The *New York Tribune* and the *Philadelphia Evening Bulletin*, Oct. 5, 1870.

Archibald hired Montreal lawyer H.J.G. McConville to investigate the case. He subpoenaed twenty witnesses and took depositions from most of them. It was far from a slam-dunk case, given the reluctance of some witnesses to testify. However, McConville, in his report to Archibald, seemed certain of the guilt of the main offender who, along with others, chased Goulet to the Red River where he drowned.

"I will immediately state to Your Excellency that the party mentioned, as the foremost in the pursuit, and the most guilty, I have no doubt, according to the testimony, it would appear, is a civilian who came from Upper Canada some time ago," wrote McConville.[13]

However, Manitoba's new recorder, Francis G. Johnson, ruled there was insufficient evidence to proceed with a prosecution. Goulet's murderers were never brought to justice. The Métis were stunned. They were also irate at what they saw as a double standard between the justice many English Protestants demanded for the execution of Thomas Scott and the lack of justice for the deaths of Goulet and others. The Ontario government issued a bounty of $5,000 for the capture of those who ordered Scott's execution. Why not the same for the people responsible for the deaths of Goulet, Tanner and others? asked *Le Métis*, Manitoba's first French newspaper, in an editorial. Did justice not extend to them as well?[14]

Meanwhile, Parliament approved a payment of $2,000 to Scott's parents as compensation for the loss of their son. No such reparation was offered to the families of Goulet or other Métis killed following the resistance.

Despite the violence and disorder that plagued the settlement, there were also reports of life improving for some in Red River—both French and English—and a return to the festive lifestyle many enjoyed prior to the resistance. The frequent Red River celebrations that had been largely paused during the uprising of 1869–70 were returning. "A gayer, a happier, a more jovial people do not exist anywhere, than the people on both sides of the Red River," *The Manitoban* wrote in January 1871. "Every night of the week we hear of balls here and balls there, and balls almost

---

[13] Report by H.J.G. McConville, Sept. 27, 1870, House of Commons sessional papers, 1871, vol. 5, no. 20, 53.

[14] *Le Métis*, Mar. 2, 1872. *Le Métis* began publishing in Manitoba in January 1872.

everywhere . . . When the dancing has once begun there is no stopping it. On it goes, one set after the other, without cessation or intermission; and the fiddlers, as if catching the general elation of spirits, fiddle as if for very life."[15]

For many, joining Canada brought greater political and economic stability to their lives. Although some were left out, many Manitobans could see a brighter future ahead. Several members of the former provisional government were elected to Manitoba's new legislative assembly or appointed to high-profile positions. Trade resumed to pre-resistance levels and new markets were opening up. The *Manitoba Free Press* began publishing in November 1872, adding a new voice to the settlement.

Manitoba held its first provincial election on December 27, 1870. Many local Métis, French and English, won seats in the new legislative assembly. John Norquay, an English-speaking Métis, was among the first twenty-four members elected to the assembly. Norquay, an eloquent speaker and a widely respected member of his community, was acclaimed in the constituency of High Bluff. He went on to become Manitoba's first Indigenous and Red River–born premier in 1878. Norquay continued the political battles his predecessors had begun in 1869–70, including over Manitoba's status within Confederation (the province did not get control of its public lands, as other provinces had, until 1930) and over controversial railway policy. Norquay successfully lobbied Prime Minister John A. Macdonald for greater transfer payments from Ottawa and negotiated Manitoba's first boundary expansion in 1881.

The right of local residents to run for public office provided Manitoba with a legislative assembly that largely reflected the broad makeup of its people. That opportunity would not have existed, at least not during the early years, had Manitoba entered Canada as a territory governed strictly by a lieutenant-governor and an appointed council. Louis Riel, who fought for provincial status, was largely responsible for ensuring Manitoba secured those democratic rights. Riel's role was recognized at the time in eastern Canada, at least among French-speaking Canadians, according to Lord

---

[15] *The Manitoban*, Jan. 21, 1871.

Dufferin, Canada's governor general in 1874. "They are united to a man in the opinion that the part played by Riel in the North West was that of a brave and spirited patriot; that it is principally to him and to those who acted with him that Manitoba owes her present privileges of self-government and her parity of rank and standing with her sister provinces."[16]

Unhappily for Riel, he was not able to participate in the democratic process he helped establish for Manitoba because of his continued exile from the province and the threat of arrest or violence against him.

Responsible government was still in its infancy in Manitoba in the 1870s. There was no premier in the first four years of the province's existence and the executive branch of government, the cabinet, was a work in progress. The lieutenant-governor was essentially the head of government during those early years. The Queen's representative governed in partnership with an elected legislative assembly and a small slate of cabinet ministers, whom he appointed. Government bills, including the establishment of the province's court system, were introduced, debated and voted on by elected members. The ability of members of the Métis community—both French and English—to hold positions in the chamber, before thousands of newcomers poured into the settlement, ensured local residents had at least some input into the development of their province.

The new provincial government had a mammoth task ahead of it: to build a government from scratch, with new laws, a court system and a taxation scheme. "You have to construct your institutions from the foundation," Archibald told the legislative assembly in his first speech from the throne on March 15, 1871. "The arrangements which have sufficed for the government of this country in the past, will no longer serve their purpose."[17] Archibald noted how "exceptional" it was for a new province with such a small population to have an elected legislative assembly. Manitoba didn't even have a conventional legislative building to conduct its affairs in the

[16] Letter from Lord Dufferin to the Earl of Carnarvon, Britain's secretary of state for the colonies, Dec. 4, 1874, House of Commons sessional papers, 1875, vol. 7, no. 11, 15.

[17] The throne speech was written by Archibald and subsequently printed in *The Manitoban* newspaper, Mar. 18, 1871.

early days. The first sessions were held in a room in the private residence of A.G.B. Bannatyne on McDermot Avenue in Winnipeg.

Archibald reminded MLAs of the significant responsibilities that lay ahead. "It will be your duty to show that the Legislature of the Dominion has not overestimated your fitness for the discharge of the very grave duties imposed upon you by your new constitution."[18]

Red River was on the cusp of change, said Archibald, transforming from a small, isolated community to a growing province that would be connected to the outside world. With telegraph service expected by the end of the year and railway lines inching ever closer, Manitoba would soon have instant communication with other parts of Canada and the U.S., he said. "Your isolation from the rest of the world, which deprived you of some advantages, protected you from many evils. That isolation is about to cease."[19]

Like most aspects of the Red River Resistance and the early days of Manitoba, the story depends on who is telling it. For recent arrivals, Canada's newest province represented opportunities—to farm and trade, to own land and raise a family, to make a new life. For some of the old settlers, many anglophones and some Métis, joining Canada meant stability, economic growth and the benefits of being part of a larger nation-state. However, for many other Métis—anglophone and francophone—it meant oppression: a loss of self-determination and dignity as many faced violence and persecution. Canada's vision was to populate the west with white settlers—a vision that often didn't include Métis or First Nations inhabitants, many of whom felt unwelcome in their own land.

---

[18] Archibald throne speech, *The Manitoban*, Mar. 18, 1871.

[19] Archibald throne speech, *The Manitoban*, Mar. 18, 1871.

CHAPTER 8

...

The Treaties

WHEN ADAMS ARCHIBALD arrived by canoe in Manitoba to assume his new position as the province's first lieutenant-governor in September 1870, tensions were running high in the settlement. It had been a tumultuous year, marked by an armed resistance, an uncertain future and threats of violence hanging over the heads of many Indigenous Manitobans. Settlers were pouring into the region at an accelerated pace, often disrupting the lives and livelihoods of First Nations. Conflict between newcomers and Indigenous people was growing.

Delays in negotiating treaties with First Nations to secure their land and sovereignty rights amplified those tensions. Despite a demand in the list of rights Red River delegates had taken to Ottawa earlier that year for the Crown to negotiate treaties with First Nations, Indigenous leaders were forced to wait. By late 1870, their patience was wearing thin.

Several First Nations Chiefs, including Henry Prince from the St. Peter's band, were the first to meet Archibald when he arrived in the new province. They greeted the lieutenant-governor at Indian Mission near the

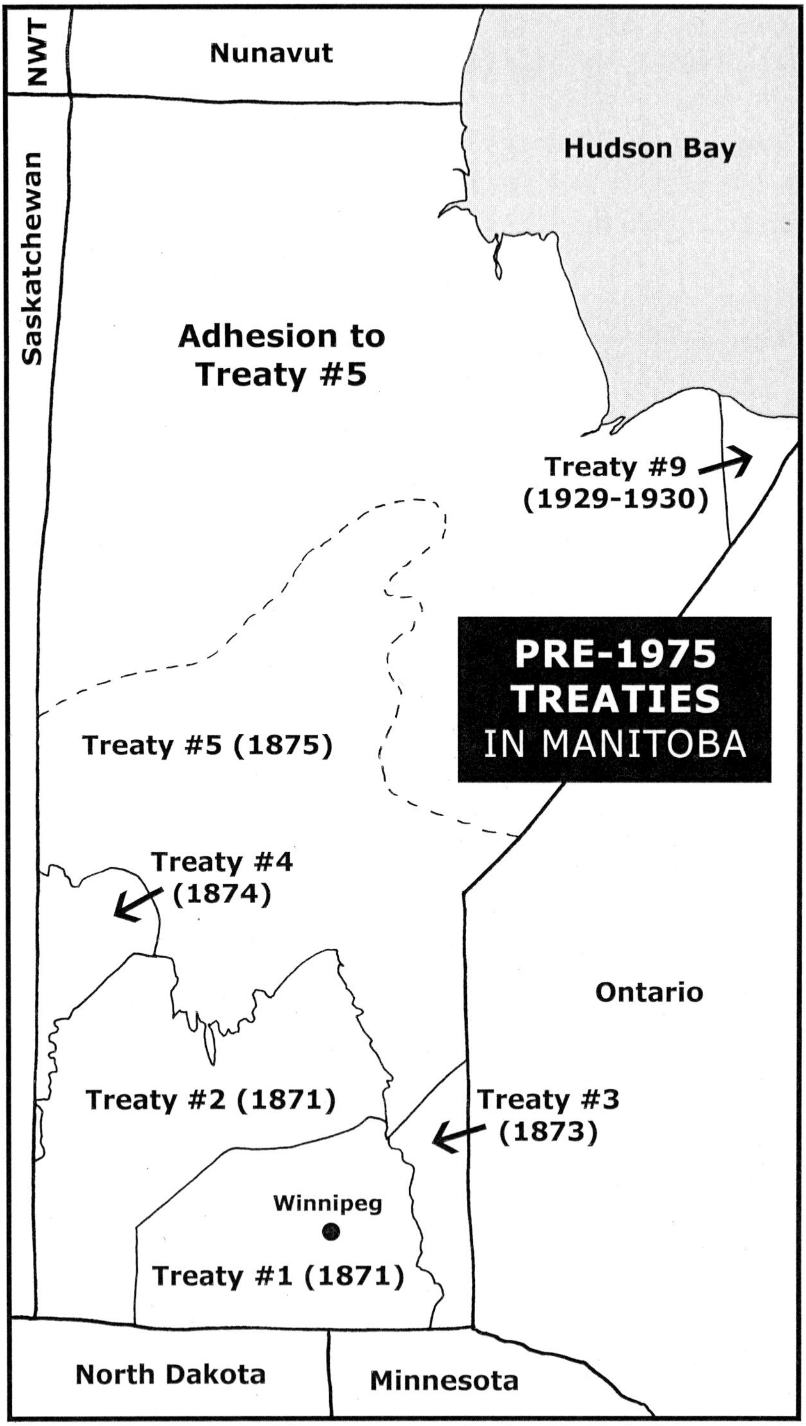

Sources: *First Nations and Treaty Areas in Manitoba* (Indigenous Services Canada) & *Pre-1975 Treaties in Manitoba* (Crown-Indigenous Relations and Northern Affairs Canada)

mouth of the Red River on his way into the settlement following a twenty-five-day journey from Ottawa through the rocky terrain of Ontario. The Chiefs were eager to begin treaty talks with the Queen's representative, a promise held out to them during the Red River Resistance while they remained largely neutral throughout the conflict. It was now time for the Crown to live up to its end of the bargain.

"The Indians in this neighbourhood are in a state of considerable excitement," Archibald wrote to federal officials in Ottawa following his arrival in Manitoba. "They are very much demoralized by the transactions of the last few months. They do not seem to see why they should not have some share of property, which they know to be in the possession of people who are not its owners."[1]

Settlers had been occupying land without obtaining official title from the Hudson's Bay Company, or permission from First Nations, for years prior to Manitoba entering Canada. But it occurred on a relatively small scale and caused little friction between First Nations and newcomers. That changed after Rupert's Land was sold to Canada. Families, land speculators and others from the east, drawn to the fertile lands of the prairies, began moving into the region in large numbers. They were offered homesteads of 160 acres per family on condition they remained for at least three years. The disruption to the lives of First Nations was growing at a rapid pace. The urgency to conclude treaties to preserve Indigenous territory and the natural resources they relied on—and to maintain peace—intensified.

While the Métis gained land concessions and the protection of their language and democratic rights through the Manitoba Act, First Nations were left on the sidelines, even though they were the original inhabitants of the land. They were promised—it's unclear by whom—that they would be rewarded for their loyalty to the Crown during "the troubles" of 1869–70 if they remained neutral during the conflict, which they largely had. "I have no doubt that, with a view to keep them quiet during the troubles, large promises were held out to them, [and] having shown themselves ready to sustain the authority of the Crown, and having refrained from pillage and

---

[1] Letter from Adams Archibald to Joseph Howe, secretary of state for the provinces, Sept. 10, 1870, House of Commons sessional papers, 1871, vol. 5, no. 20, 11.

disorder, they feel that they have claims for consideration and remuneration, and it is impossible not to admit that from their point of view, there is some justice in their claims," wrote Archibald.[2]

The lieutenant-governor also remarked in his first correspondence to Ottawa following his arrival at Fort Garry that he was "impressed" that First Nations communities had refrained from attacking Wolseley's troops as they travelled to Red River. "We have reason to congratulate ourselves that they have proved loyal to the Crown and resisted the attempts which were made to seduce them from their allegiance."[3] Archibald did not say who might have attempted to seduce them or for what purpose.

William McDougall, the lieutenant-governor designate who had been holed up at Pembina during the fall of 1869, had made commitments of some kind to First Nations Chiefs during the weeks he spent at the U.S. border. McDougall was prevented from crossing the border, but he had supporters in Red River who couriered correspondence for him between Pembina and Red River. In a letter to HBC governor William Mactavish at Upper Fort Garry, McDougall said he was in communication with a Chief by the name of Pegwis. It is unknown who that was, but it may have been Chief Henry Prince, the son of the late Chief Peguis, one of five Chiefs who negotiated the Selkirk Treaty in 1817. In the correspondence, McDougall wrote that he had promised to meet with First Nations leaders at Fort Garry to discuss land rights. First Nations, he said, had been persuaded by "loyal persons having influence with them" that the Métis resistance could negatively impact their interests:

> I have received a friendly letter from the Indian chief "Pegwis," who lives at Winnipeg, in which he strongly condemns the conduct of the French half-breeds. He reminds me that they come from my own country, and are "very bad men." He wishes to see me, to shake

[2] Archibald to Howe, Sept. 21, 1870, House of Commons sessional papers, 1871, vol. 5, no. 20, 18.

[3] Archibald to Howe, Sept. 3, 1870, House of Commons sessional papers, 1871, vol. 5, no. 20, 9.

> hands and bargain about his land. He has offered his services to the Canadians in the settlement to put down Riel and his party, evidently foreseeing that if they got the mastery, the Indian title to the land in Assiniboine will not be treated with much respect or realize much profit.
>
> I have returned a verbal answer to his letter, expressing the most friendly feelings towards him and his people, and my desire to see them at Fort Garry as soon as possible. I though it better to put nothing in writing, and indeed to say nothing that could be construed into an invitation to the Indians to arm or attack any class of the inhabitants, not even those now under arms and in a state of insurrection. It is very satisfactory to find that the Indians in all directions, and under different chiefs, are well disposed, and unwilling to give any aid to the French half-breeds. I have taken pains, through the agency of loyal persons having influence with them, to arouse apprehensions of the Indians in reference to the annexation features of the half-breed movement, and its effect upon them and their land claims. They have been quick to perceive that the outbreak bodes no good to them, and they cannot therefore be seduced into any kind of sympathy with it. This fact is already producing a marked effect upon the plans and operations of the insurgents.[4]

McDougall was careful "to put nothing in writing" and made verbal commitments instead to meet with the Chief to "bargain about his land." Those verbal promises were likely made through one of his intermediaries.

On November 1, 1869, while at Pembina, McDougall met with a Chippewa Chief by the name of Kewetaosh. The Chief and members of his community sought a meeting with McDougall to discuss land issues. Following a pipe-smoking ceremony—which the lieutenant-governor designate described in detail in a letter to Joseph Howe—Kewetaosh informed McDougall that he and other nations had claims to territory in the area and

---

[4] Letter from William McDougall to Joseph Howe, Nov. 29, 1869, House of Commons sessional papers, 1870, vol. 5, no. 12, 65–66.

asked what the Crown's plans were with respect to those lands. He also asked if the Crown had bought First Nations territory from the Hudson's Bay Company.

> He then proceeded to lay claim to the country from Pembina to the Assiniboine, and from the high lands on the West to the Lake of the Woods. He said his ancestors had never sold their title to any part of it, they had only lent as much as a man could see under a horse's belly on both sides of the river to the Company[5]; and he now wanted to know what I was going to do with his land. He repeated his desire to be on good terms with me, and said that neither he nor his band had anything to do with the movements or designs of the French half-breeds.[6]

McDougall said he produced a map of the area and asked Kewetaosh to point out which lands they claimed to control. Kewetaosh replied that he and other First Nations Chiefs from the area, including a Chief "Peguwis,"[7] had agreed the previous winter to a division of land. McDougall agreed to negotiate with Kewetaosh at a later date at Fort Garry and asked the Chief to bring a list of his band's families and their names to the negotiations. It does not appear any specific promises were made except that the Crown was willing to negotiate some type of land deals with First Nations, through treaty or otherwise. McDougall was unable to carry out negotiations with First Nations because he was denied access to the territory and forced to return to Ottawa. However, he did commit to talks with at least two First Nations Chiefs.

Like the Métis, First Nations objected to the sale of Rupert's Land to Canada without their consent. They were neither consulted about the transaction nor offered compensation. Many Indigenous leaders saw the

---

[5] A reference to the Selkirk Treaty of 1817.

[6] Letter from William McDougall to Joseph Howe, Nov. 5, 1869, House of Commons sessional papers, 1870, vol. 5, no. 12, 18.

[7] Yet another version of the spelling by McDougall that is likely *Peguis*.

land transfer as illegitimate. That grievance was expressed numerous times by First Nations Chiefs during treaty negotiations following Manitoba's entry into Confederation.

Archibald was given instructions by Ottawa to "establish friendly relations" with First Nations and determine how best to clear the way for Europeans and Canadians to settle the west, "whether by treaty or otherwise."[8] The federal government was keenly aware that treaties were necessary to avoid a clash between settlers and First Nations. However, government officials were less interested in fair compensation for Indigenous people for settlers having intruded on their territory—or in coexisting with them as equal stewards of the land—and more focused on finding ways to get them out of the way to facilitate the settlement of newcomers. They knew treaties, including the allocation of reserve land, would be necessary to achieve that goal.

Adams Archibald was a former provincial politician in Nova Scotia and a staunch supporter of Confederation. He was recruited by John A. Macdonald to enter federal politics and appointed secretary of state for the provinces in 1867. He resigned from that post amid growing opposition in his home province to joining Canada. However, he later won a federal by-election in 1869 in Colchester, Nova Scotia. As a member of Parliament, Archibald spoke favourably of the Manitoba Act during House of Commons debates and agreed to serve as the province's first lieutenant-governor.

Archibald was a seasoned politician who picked up on the lay of the land quickly following his arrival. After consulting with Chiefs and other leaders in the community, he was aware of the urgency around treaty talks. However, he delayed negotiations until the following year, telling Prince and other Chiefs he needed time to establish a new provincial government at Upper Fort Garry. He promised he would summon them for talks in the spring. In the meantime, he attempted to quell tensions between First Nations and non-Indigenous settlers around Indian Mission. He was under

---

8 Letter from Edmund Allen Meredith, undersecretary of state for the provinces, to Adams Archibald, Aug. 4, 1870, House of Commons sessional papers, 1871, vol. 5, no. 20, 8.

pressure to persuade the nations to "disperse to their hunting grounds" and avoid "hostile collision between them and the people," he wrote in a letter to Joseph Howe.[9] He discouraged them from meeting with him at Fort Garry.

Archibald provided the Chiefs with ammunition and gun flints, a few bags of flour, tobacco and tea to encourage them to leave. He also used the fear of a smallpox outbreak in nearby Portage la Prairie as further inducement to relocate. "The Indians are in great terror of this disease, which proves so fatal to persons of their race, and I am in hopes they will, for their own sake and for the sake of the neighbourhood, immediately disperse," Archibald further wrote to Howe. Most did. The lieutenant-governor had bought himself some time. In the meantime, he strongly urged the federal government to begin treaty talks the following year. After waiting through the winter and spring of 1870–71 for the Crown to make good on its solemn pledge, First Nations returned in large numbers the following summer to negotiate the first in what would be a historic series of nation-to-nation treaties.

TREATY 1

Hundreds of Anishinaabe and Swampy Cree poured into the grounds of Lower Fort Garry in late July 1871, many arriving by foot or on horseback with their families. Some had travelled from as far away as the United States border. They set up birchbark lodges and tents outside the Hudson's Bay trading post, located along the banks of the Red River, about 19 miles north of Winnipeg. Women baked bread and made tea while children ran about. The sounds of chanting in a low tone and the hammering of a frying pan filled the air, signaling a game of gambling was about to begin. The encampment formed a semicircle outside the fort. In the middle, First Nations Chiefs held council.[10]

These were the ancestors of First Nations from Brokenhead Ojibway, Long Plain, Peguis, Roseau River, Sagkeeng, Sandy Bay and Swan Lake.

---

[9] Archibald to Joseph Howe, secretary of state for the provinces, Sept. 17, 1870, House of Commons sessional papers, 1871, vol. 5, no. 20, 15.

[10] *The Manitoban*, Aug. 29, 1871.

They came to negotiate a treaty with the Crown. First Nations were accustomed to treaty-making among tribes prior to the arrival of European settlers. Many negotiated pacts with the Hudson's Bay Company to secure trade relations and to grant the company access to Indigenous territory. While British colonies had negotiated treaties with First Nations in the east prior to Confederation in 1867, this would be the first formal alliance under the new country of Canada.

Negotiations were scheduled to begin July 25, 1871, outside the fort. Indian commissioner Wemyss Simpson was chosen by Ottawa to negotiate on behalf of Canada. He arrived at Lower Fort Garry on July 24. Archibald represented the Crown. Simpson came with orders from Ottawa to "extinguish Indian title" to lands required for settlement in the Northwest, at the lowest possible cost to government. Both sides were eager to negotiate a deal.

Joseph Howe, secretary of state for the provinces, wrote to Simpson:

> The powers intrusted to you are large, and they should be used with constant reference to the responsibility which the Government owes to Parliament and to the country for the judicious and economical expenditure of the funds and supplies in trusted to your charge. It should therefore be your endeavor to secure the session of the lands upon terms as favorable as possible to the Government, not going as far as the maximum sum hereafter named unless it be found impossible to obtain the object for a less amount.[11]

The goal: to get land from First Nations as cheaply as possible. The maximum annual compensation was $12 per family of five, wrote Howe, who cautioned Simpson that whatever compensation he offered First Nations would likely serve as a template for future treaties. Simpson said the highest price paid to First Nations for the "finest lands" in Quebec or Ontario in past treaties seldom, if ever, exceeded "four dollars per head per annum," or

[11] Letter from Joseph Howe to Wemyss Simpson, May 6, 1871, Report of the Indian Branch of the Department of Secretary of State for the Provinces, House of Commons sessional papers, 1872, vol. 7, no. 22, 6.

$20 per family of five. Howe urged Simpson to bargain below that. "In fixing this amount, you must not lose sight of the fact that it cannot fail to have an important bearing on the arrangements to be made subsequently with the tribes further West."[12]

Howe was less specific about the size of the reserves or how they should be used. However, he did point out that reserve lands should be seen as tools to "civilize" First Nations, a colonial theme that hung like a dark cloud over all treaty talks and underscored the perceived racial superiority of non-Indigenous settlers. "One part of your duty, and by no means the least important, will be to select desirable reserves for the use of the Indians themselves, with a view to the gradual introduction of those agencies[13] which in Canada [have] operated so beneficially in promoting settlement and civilization among the Indians."[14]

First Nations were aware of Ottawa's desire to avoid violent clashes with Indigenous people and to settle the west as peaceably as possible. At the same time, the Chiefs and their representatives sought to retain and protect as much of their traditional territory and way of life as they could while demanding compensation for land shared with newcomers. The inevitability of European settlement was not lost on them; their goal was to seek peaceful coexistence with newcomers. Yet many communities were already resisting the encroachment of white settlers, who were occupying land and cutting timber on First Nations territory without their consent, especially around the Portage la Prairie area. The Portage band in that area posted a sign on the door of a local church informing settlers to stop harvesting their trees.

The federal government viewed Indigenous people in the west largely as a threat. They feared "Indian wars" and further clashes between First Nations and non-Indigenous settlers. It was one of the reasons Ottawa had deployed troops to the area less than a year earlier. Despite the official

---

12 Howe to Simpson, May 6, 1871, 6.

13 Howe was presumably referring to the federal government's desire to persuade First Nations to take up farming on allocated reserve land.

14 Howe to Simpson, May 6, 1871, 7.

position of the federal government that sending a military expedition to Red River the previous year was solely a "mission of peace," Archibald's written instructions from the federal government confirmed otherwise: "You are aware that the unsettled state of things in the North-West has compelled the Queen's Government to despatch a military force into that country with a view to protect Her Majesty's subjects from the possible intrusion of roving bands of Indians by whom they are surrounded, and to give stability to the civil government which it will be your duty to organize."[15]

Canada was compelled by the British government to negotiate treaties with First Nations prior to settlement. It was a requirement under the terms of acquiring Rupert's Land from the HBC. The federal government was also obligated to do so under the Royal Proclamation of 1763, issued by King George III. The historic document stipulates that Indigenous land can only be obtained by the Crown through treaties. Settlers were prohibited from purchasing or acquiring territory directly from First Nations. Treaty talks had to occur in public settings and both sides had to be properly represented. Given those legal requirements, First Nations had some leverage at the negotiating table, but it was limited. While the Crown had a duty to negotiate in good faith, the historical record shows its commitment to that duty was dubious at best.

One of the starkest examples of that inequity was the frequency with which Archibald and Simpson threatened First Nations with an ultimatum: If Indigenous leaders did not accept what Ottawa was offering, settlers would occupy their lands in any event and First Nations would be left with nothing. Archibald told the Chiefs it was "God's will" that the Northwest should be settled by newcomers and used for farming "to raise great crops for all his children."[16] Ottawa's offer may not have been a take-it-or-leave-it proposition, but it wasn't far off. First Nations had some agency, but Crown negotiators had the upper hand, which they used to their advantage at every opportunity. "White people will come here and cultivate it (the land) under any circumstances," Archibald told the Chiefs during negotiations. "No power on earth can prevent it."

---

[15] Meredith to Archibald, August 4, 1870, 6.

That power imbalance was obvious to First Nations Chiefs. "I know our great mother the Queen is strong, and that we cannot keep back her power no more than we can keep back the sun," Chief Ayee-ta-pe-pe-tung, representing the Portage band, told Simpson during the fourth day of talks. "If therefore the commissioner wants the land, let him take it."

Ultimatums were not the only tactics used by Crown officials to dominate talks. Archibald brought troops with him as a display of colonial authority, even though the negotiations were supposed to be carried out in a spirit of peace and diplomacy. "Military display has always a great effect on savages, and the presence, even of a few troops, will have a good tendency," he wrote several days before talks began. Even the physical positioning of the two sides—Crown officials under an awning shielded from the elements and First Nations leaders in the open air, rained on at one point during discussions—was symbolic of the lopsided talks.

Still, Indigenous leaders had some bargaining power, which they exploited as far as they could, making what Simpson and Archibald claimed at one point to be "outrageous" demands. Government officials knew Treaty 1 would set a precedent for subsequent treaty talks and sought to limit concessions as much as possible. "The terms we now agree upon will probably shape the arrangements we shall have to make with all the Indians between the Red River and the Rocky Mountains,"[17] Archibald wrote to Ottawa.

Two days after negotiations had been scheduled to start, representatives from both sides arrived. The stage was set. History-making was about to begin.

---

[16] *The Manitoban* newspaper published extensive coverage of Treaty 1 talks; it remains one of the most important sources documenting the proceedings. While not entirely neutral (the unnamed reporter or reporters often displayed a bias in favour of the Crown), it is the closest thing to an independent record that exists. Indian commissioner Wemyss Simpson vouched for the accuracy of the newspaper coverage and included copies of the stories in his records. Unless otherwise noted, quotations of the proceedings are taken from *The Manitoban*, July 29 and August 5–12, 1871 editions.

[17] Letter from Adams Archibald to secretary of state for the provinces, July 22, 1871, in Alexander Morris, *The Treaties of Canada with the Indians of Manitoba and the North-West Territories* (Toronto: Willing & Williamson, 1880), 32.

JULY 27, 1871

Negotiations began with a spectacular opening ceremony by the Anishinaabe inside Lower Fort Garry. Simpson, Archibald and a large gathering of local residents and government officials were among the spectators. *The Manitoban* reported:

> The performances, between ribbons, feathers, paint and clothing, exhibited all the colors of the rainbow. There were two orchestras, half women and half men, one set playing for one style of dancing, and the other for another and very different one. The band and performers were all seated on the grass, and the commissioner, lieutenant-governor and party, and a great crowd formed the spectators. Some of the chiefs and braves were in the most fashionable style of dress—that is, dressed as little as possible; having merely breechcloths on; others had buffalo horns, &c., on their heads, while bears' claws, and similar remembrancers were plentifully scattered through the group.

Talks began at 4:00 p.m. following the opening ceremony. Simpson, who had stepped down earlier that year as a Conservative member of Parliament to accept the position of Indian commissioner, was dressed in military attire. He was granted officer status in the militia for the treaty talks to enhance his appearance of authority. Archibald, in his Windsor suit, was accompanied by his aide-de-camp. The two government officials "were screened from the sun by an awning, under which several ladies and officers also found seats," *The Manitoban* reported. "From the far end of the camp, the Indians moved to meet the commissioner en masse, the chiefs occupying the foremost rank." The Chiefs sat in the front row. Among them were Henry Prince from the St. Peter's band (Peguis), Tachou-chous from Fort Alexander, Red Deer from Brokenhead, and Yellow Quill from the Portage band. Interpreters were present for both sides. Archibald and Simpson did most of the talking on the first day. The Chiefs listened.

"Your Great Mother wishes the good of all races under her sway," Archibald said during his opening address, invoking the authority of Queen Victoria, the reigning British monarch, while appealing to the cultural importance of kinship among his Indigenous audience. "She wishes her red children, as well as her white people, to be happy and contented. She wished them to live in comfort." Archibald laid out in broad strokes what government was offering: Newcomers would arrive in the Northwest to farm and occupy unspecified amounts of territory, while the federal government would set aside land, called reserves, for the exclusive use of Indigenous communities. Those reserves could be used for farming, or any other purpose, "by you and your children forever," he said. "She will not allow the white man to intrude upon these lots. She will make rules to keep them for you, so that as long as the sun shall shine there shall be no Indian who has not a place that he can call his home, where he can go and pitch his camp, or, if he chooses, build his house and till his land."

Prince, Yellow Quill and the other Chiefs could not have known it at the time, but what Archibald said next was a foreshadowing of the paternalistic relationship and assimilative policies that would develop between Canada and Indigenous people over the following century and beyond. The Queen would like "her red children" to live more like white people. "She would like them to adopt the habits of the whites, to till land and raise food, and store it up against a time of want," Archibald said. "She thinks this would be the best thing for her red children to do; that it would make them safer from famine and sickness, and make their homes more comfortable."

Adopting "civilized" habits was associated with race—the white race. It became the cornerstone of a relationship of presumed white superiority between Canada and Indigenous people. It led to attempts over subsequent generations to extinguish First Nations, Métis and Inuit as a people using coercive assimilative methods, such as forced attendance at residential schools and the banning of Indigenous cultural rituals. Those government policies contradicted what Archibald promised at the time: that First Nations would not be forced to assimilate into white culture. The Queen promised they could continue living as they always had, as long as they agreed to share the land with newcomers, he said.

"This she leaves to your choice, and you need not live like the white man unless you can be persuaded to do so with your own free will," said Archibald. "When you have made your treaty, you will still be free to hunt over much of the land included in the treaty. Much of it is rocky, and unfit for cultivation; much of it that is wooded, is beyond the places where the white man will require to go, at all events, for some time to come."

What the approximately one thousand Indigenous people present during Treaty 1 negotiations did not know was that five years later, the federal government would pass the Indian Act. The legislation, at first an amalgamation of existing "Indian policies" already in place, would become the main instrument used by Ottawa to dominate every aspect of First Nations' lives, with the express intent of extinguishing their language, culture and way of life. The statute and its subsequent amendments, which made First Nations wards of the state, was a wholesale violation of what First Nations Chiefs were promised during the summer of 1871 at the Stone Fort.

Simpson followed Archibald with his opening remarks. He reaffirmed most of what the lieutenant-governor had said, but also sought to lower the Chiefs' expectations. The government was offering First Nations land for farming, but they should not expect "immense reserves" beyond what was needed for agricultural purposes. Reserve sizes would be one of the main sticking points during negotiations. "The government will give to the Indians reserves amply sufficient," said Simpson. "The different bands will get such quantities of land as will be sufficient for their use in adopting the habits of the whites, should they choose to do so." Adopting the habits of the whites was a phrase repeated often during treaty talks.

Until then, the Chiefs had sat and listened. Chief Henry Prince was the first to come forward. He shook hands with the commissioner and the lieutenant-governor and said in his language, "It is many years ago since I first heard such gentlemen would come among us; but this is the first time I have heard the Queen's representative. I am very much obliged to His Excellency for the kind advice he has given us, and in hearing the commissioner this evening. I feel that we heard the Queen's voice. That is all I have got to say at present. I will go back to the camp and select a spokesman." Chief Ayee-ta-pe-pe-tung was less optimistic: "This day is like a darkness to me and I am not prepared to answer," he said, after shaking hands with the commissioner. "All is darkness to me how to plan for the future welfare of my grandchildren." Simpson promised to send tobacco to the camp. The meeting was adjourned to 10:00 the next morning.

JULY 28, 1871

Lower Fort Garry was not just a Hudson's Bay Company trading post in 1871. It also served as a jail. Among those in custody during treaty talks were four Indigenous men from the Portage band who had been found guilty, under a recently passed provincial law, of deserting their posts as boatmen with the HBC. They couldn't pay their fines so were jailed for forty days. Ayee-ta-pe-pe-tung, "a tall old brave, who was naked all but the breech-clout, and had his body smeared with white earth," said he could not negotiate while his men were jailed and requested they be released. "I can scarcely hear the Queen's words," he said, holding an eagle's wing. "An obstacle is in the way. Some of my children are in that building." He was not challenging the legitimacy of the law, he said, but wanted his men released. "I hold my own very sacred, and therefore, could not work while my child is sitting in the dark."

Archibald agreed "as a matter of favour, not as a matter of right," and only after a lecture about how people of all races were equal under the law and Indigenous people would have to obey the laws of the land. "If a man does wrong, whether a white man or an Indian, he has to suffer for it," said Archibald. "If a white man makes a bargain with an Indian, and does not fulfil it, the Queen will punish the white. If, on the other hand, an Indian does wrong to an Indian or white man, the law is the same, he will be punished." Archibald ordered the release of the Saulteaux men. "The discharge of the prisoners had an excellent effect," he wrote to Ottawa the next day.

Not everything discussed during negotiations was recorded; much of it has been lost to history. There are countless examples of undocumented proceedings during the Treaty 1 talks. For instance, after Archibald agreed to release the four Saulteaux men from prison, Wa-sus koo-koon, a spokesman for a First Nations community between Pembina and Fort Garry, wanted to know more about what the Queen intended for his people. Simpson responded, and James McKay, an English-speaking Métis who served as one of the interpreters for the Crown, "entered into a very full explanation in Indian," *The Manitoban* reported. But the content of that explanation was not reported. It was a significant omission, considering federal negotiators and their interpreters acknowledged, following Treaty

1 negotiations, that many verbal commitments made by the Crown were not included in the text of the treaty. It is unknown what commitments McKay may have promised in that instance, or in others.

While the Chiefs and their spokesmen bargained hard with Crown officials and peppered them with questions about treaty details, they also maintained friendly relations throughout the negotiations. Their approach was conciliatory and respectful. Ka-kee-ga-by-ness, the Chief from Fort Alexander, "a little man wearing a stove-pipe hat of very considerable elevation," told the commissioner he saluted the Great Mother and was satisfied with what he had heard so far. "I take all my Great Mother's children here by the hand and welcome them," he said. "I am very much pleased that myself and my children are to be clothed by the Queen and on that account welcome every white man into the country."

Prior to the end of the day's deliberations, a daughter of one of the First Nations Chiefs "wearing a couple of medals and in years being decidedly the shady side of fifty," came forward in an act of kindness and shook hands with both Archibald and Simpson. After she turned and walked away, she decided handshakes were not enough to express her friendship. "She advanced to the front again and kissed both the great men amid the hearty laughter and applause of over 1,000 spectators, red and white," *The Manitoban* reported.

Meanwhile, Simpson provided further details of what the Crown was offering. In addition to reserves set aside for farming, Ottawa would provide each Indigenous person with an annuity, in cash or goods, in perpetuity. The opening offer was $12 per family of five, the high end of what Joseph Howe had instructed. The size of the reserves would be determined in consultation with Indigenous leaders, Simpson explained. Reserves would be separate from unoccupied land, which could still be used as hunting grounds. The Chiefs said they needed to consult further. Talks resumed the following day.

JULY 29, 1871

Several Chiefs, including Ka-ma-twa-kan-nas-nin, representing Fort Alexander and Oak Point, and Wa-sus-koo-koon speaking for First Nations between Pembina and Fort Garry, made their first counteroffers. They proposed specific reserve sizes, some of which were close to 200 square miles. At the same time, Ayee-ta-pe-pe-tung cautioned his own fellow Chiefs not to disclose their proposed reserve sizes before they heard what the Crown was offering, advice that they ultimately did not heed. Ayee-ta-pe-pe-tung was the only Chief who withheld his proposed reserve size. He told Simpson his intention was not to offend. "If I used any improper language, I did not mean to be insulting," he said. "I want, first, to see what you are offering and then I'll tell you my offer."

What Simpson was offering was far less than what the Chiefs had in mind. Government was willing to set aside modest areas of land for reserves. But what the Chiefs were proposing was out of the question, said Simpson. "If all these lands are to be reserved, I would like to know what you have to sell," he told the Chiefs. He said the demands were "so preposterous" that if granted, there would be virtually no land left to cede for settlers. He urged the Chiefs to reconsider. Archibald reported to Ottawa later that day that it appeared the Chiefs "misunderstood" the government's intentions. "When we met this morning, the Indians were invited to state their wishes as to the reserves, they were to say how much they thought would be sufficient, and whether they wished them all in one or in several places," Archibald wrote. "In defining the limits of their reserves, so far as we could see, they wished to have about two-thirds of the province." The amount of land the Chiefs were requesting "amounted to about three townships per Indian, and included the greater part of the settled portions of the province," Simpson wrote to Ottawa several days later. "When their answer came it proved to contain demands of such an exorbitant nature, that much time was spent in reducing their terms to a basis upon which an arrangement could be made."

What the government had in mind was 160 acres per family—a "generous" offer that would give First Nations a head start over white settlers, Archibald said. Indigenous people in the east had signed similar treaties and were "enjoying all the rights and privileges of white men," he told the leaders. The Chiefs were urged to "dismiss all nonsense" about wanting large reserves. For the first time during talks, the threat was raised that if

First Nations didn't take what was on the table, they would get nothing in the future. "We told them that whether they wished it or not, immigrants would come in and fill up the country," Archibald wrote to Ottawa. "That every year from this one twice as many in number as their whole people there assembled would pour into the province and in a little while would spread all over it, and that now was the time for them to come to an arrangement that would secure homes and annuities for themselves and their children."[18] The Chiefs were told to take the rest of the weekend to consider government's offer and return Monday with an answer. There were no talks on Sunday.

JULY 31, 1871

After three days of talks, there was little consensus between the Chiefs and government officials. Simpson believed he was close to a deal but clearly misread the Chiefs. "As far as I can judge, I am inclined to think that the Indians will accept these terms,"[19] he wrote on July 30. However, he was faced mostly with opposition on the fourth day of negotiations. Ayee-ta-pe-pe-tung said he saw little in what government was offering that would benefit his children. "God gave me this land you are speaking to me about, and it has kept me well to this day," he told Simpson, adding he was prepared to walk away from the table. "After I showed you what I meant to keep for a reserve, you continued to make it smaller and smaller. Now, I will go home today, to my own property, without being treated with. You (the commissioner) can please yourself... Let the Queen's subjects go on my land if they choose. I give them liberty. Let them rob me. I will go home without treating."

Archibald tried a new tactic. He suggested First Nations in Manitoba didn't have a legitimate claim to the land in question because their tribes, the Chippewas (another name for the Saulteaux, who are Anishinaabe)

---

18 Letter from Adams Archibald to secretary of state for the provinces, July 29, 1871, in Morris, *The Treaties of Canada*, 34.

19 Letter from Wemyss Simpson to secretary of state for the provinces, July 30, 1870, in Morris, *Treaties of Canada*, 36.

were originally from the east. They had not occupied the territory a hundred years earlier, he said. The implication was that the Anishinaabe's connection to the land was tenuous. "When the buffalo went westward, the Crees [*sic*] went with them; and the Chippewas, finding the land unoccupied, came in and stopped here," Archibald said. "But they have no right to the land beyond that." Besides, what Ottawa was offering First Nations in Manitoba was similar, or even more generous, than what Indigenous people had received through treaties in the east, Archibald said. "Is the Indian in this country so much better than the Indian of the Lake of the Woods, or Lake Superior, that he must receive better terms?" he said rhetorically. The lieutenant-governor told the Chiefs that when the white man came to Manitoba to cultivate land, they got nothing from government, whereas a First Nations person got reserve land and annual payments. That, of course, was not entirely accurate; under the Dominion Lands Act passed the following year, many non-Indigenous newcomers were given land grants by government.

Ayee-ta-pe-pe-tung challenged Archibald on his assertion First Nations in Manitoba did not have a true claim to the territory, prompting Simpson to intervene. The commissioner suggested some "evil bird was whispering in council." Negotiations grew tense.

Both Simpson and Archibald continued to threaten that it would be "unwise" and "foolish" for the Chiefs to turn down the Crown's offer, repeating that "white people" would be coming into the province no matter what. Without a treaty, First Nations would be left with no land to cultivate.

Wa-sus-koo-koon raised an important point: What would happen when First Nations families had more children and their communities grew? Where would their children's land be? Archibald told him that the government would accommodate that growth by giving First Nations more land as required. "Whenever his children get more numerous than they are now, they will be provided for further west," said Archibald, according to *The Manitoban*. "Whenever the reserves are found too small, the government will sell the land and give the Indians land elsewhere." It was an unusual offer, considering Archibald had no authority to promise more land than what Simpson had offered. It was one of many oral promises made during the talks that were not included in the written text of the treaty (some were added in 1875 in what became known as the "outside promises," but not all). In the end, the commitment to provide additional land to accommodate growing Indigenous communities was never fulfilled by the federal government.

Negotiations continued throughout the day. Finally, a small breakthrough: Ayee-ta-pe-pe-tung said he would agree to a treaty if the annuity was increased from $12 per family of five to $3 per person. Simpson seized on it immediately. "I take you at your word at once," said the commissioner. "The additional sum is not large, and I will take it on myself to make the amount up to $3 a head. You will get the amount of reserves we offer, and the annuity you have asked, and we will finish the matter at once." But not everyone was satisfied. Ayee-ta-pe-pe-tung said he spoke only for his own nation. Simpson, growing impatient, threatened to end negotiations unless the Chiefs came to an agreement the next day.

AUGUST 2, 1871

There were no talks on August 1 because of bad weather. Archibald also had business to attend to in Winnipeg. As a result, both sides had additional time to consider the other's position. Negotiations resumed on August 2. Simpson, growing impatient, now demanded a final answer. This would be the final day of sitting, he said. Considering the historic and far-reaching implications of entering into a treaty of this magnitude, it hardly seemed appropriate to rush talks. However, Simpson wanted a deal and he was under immense pressure from Ottawa to secure one as quickly as possible. He had no appetite for protracted talks.

The Chiefs still had questions—lots of them. Chief Henry Prince said he wanted to know how government would treat Indigenous people and their land under the treaty. "The land cannot speak for itself," he said. "We have to speak for it and want to know fully how you are going to treat our children." He also wanted to know how First Nations were supposed to take up farming if they had no equipment and livestock. "The Queen wishes the Indians to cultivate the ground," said Prince. "They cannot scratch it—work it with their fingers. What assistance will they get if they settle down?" Archibald said the Queen was willing to help First Nations any way she could, including providing a school and a schoolmaster for each reserve and plows and harrows for those willing to farm.

The Chiefs made another counteroffer: In addition, they wanted clothes for their children every spring and fall, fully furnished homes when requested, cattle, buggies for the Chiefs, councillors and braves, hunting supplies, and tax-free status on reserves. "If you grant this request," Wa-sus-koo-koon said, "I will say you have shown kindness to me and to the Indians." Simpson's reply drew laughter from both sides, including from Wa-sus-koo-koon. "I am proud of being an Englishman," said Simpson. "But if Indians are going to be dealt with in this way, I will take my coat off and change places with the speaker, for it would by far better to be an Indian."

AUGUST 3, 1871

Whatever led to an agreement on the final day of talks on August 3 is missing from the historical record. The Portage band and its Chief abandoned the negotiations before the end of the previous day. Other Chiefs were reportedly considering doing the same. Treaty 1 negotiations were on the brink of collapse. However, in a miraculous turn of events, James McKay, the influential Métis who acted as an interpreter for the Crown, brought the two sides together the following day. What he said or promised First Nations Chiefs is unknown, but it led to a surprising and successful conclusion: the two sides agreed on a treaty. "All the Indians met His Excellency and the Commissioner today in better humour," *The Manitoban* reported. "The Commissioner said he understood they were disposed to sign the treaty . . ."

In addition to what was agreed to thus far, including 160 acres of reserve land per family, a $3 per person annuity, farm implements, and a school on each reserve, each person would receive a one-time $3 "present," each reserve would get a pair of oxen, and buggies (light spring wagons) would be supplied to each Chief. "This gave general satisfaction, and the treaty was soon signed, sealed and delivered, with all due formality," *The Manitoban* continued. "The ceremony was witnessed by a large crowd of spectators."

It is unclear exactly what else was agreed to. Given the language barriers, it is also unknown whether the Chiefs understood everything that ended up in the written text of the treaty. Nevertheless, it appears that common ground was found on how to share the land Canadian settlers would soon occupy. The specifics, and the interpretation, of the agreement would be the subject of vigorous debate for generations.

Treaty 1 was important for many reasons. It established a precedent for subsequent numbered treaties, including Treaty 2, negotiated later that month at Manitoba Post, an HBC trading post on the west shore of Lake Manitoba, with First Nations residing in what is today central Manitoba. It was also Canada's first treaty with First Nations since it had become a country. It was seen in eastern Canada as a critical development that allowed for the settlement of the west. Manitoba's entry into Canada was not complete without it.

The *Kingston Daily News* in Ontario reported the following on August 29, 1871, less than a month after Treaty 1 was concluded:

> Lengthy despatches have been received from Lieutenant Governor Archibald, of Manitoba, giving particulars of the negotiations with Indians. Before the treaty was concluded a number of Ontario emigrants who settled in the vicinity of Portage la Prairie had been warned by the Indians against taking possession of the lands, but they have now been able to settle upon them and proceed with their cultivation. The conclusion of this treaty was absolutely necessary before the province could be settled, and is, of course, important.

The territory Canada claimed it took possession of from First Nations through treaties was valuable land. Indian commissioners often attempted to downplay the worth of the land when negotiating treaties with First Nations to minimize how much they had to pay in compensation through annuities, one-time "gifts" and in reserve land. However, it was clear the land in question contained an abundance of rich natural resources and fertile soil newcomers could exploit, especially outside the "postage stamp" province of Manitoba. The richness of the land and the agricultural opportunities it represented became a selling point in eastern Canada to encourage people to move west, as reported in one newspaper article:

> The treaty negotiation with the Indians by Governor Archibald and Mr. Simpson is regarded with the utmost satisfaction by every one. It places at our immediate disposal an immense tract of land outside the province, some of which is firmer than any which can be found in Manitoba. The crops this summer have been splendid, the average yield of wheat bring fully 35 bushels to the acre. One man had 300 bushels of wheat of five acres of land, or about 60 bushels to the acre. Money is plentiful in the province and socially and politically the people appear to be in a very prosperous and contented state.[20]

INTERPRETATION OF THE TREATIES

Many Indigenous Elders argue that their ancestors never agreed to cede or surrender their land. The numbered treaties were agreements with the Crown to share the land and to live in peaceful coexistence with newcomers, they maintain. Part of that understanding, passed down through generations of oral history, is based on the sacred relationship Indigenous people have with the land: people don't own land, they live in harmony with it. "The land is a living entity, it has its own intelligence," said Sagkeeng First Nations Elder David Courchene in a 2021 interview with the *Winnipeg Free Press*. "That is what the elders and the nations of our people have always lived by."[21]

But the federal government's position at the time was that Treaty 1, and all the subsequent numbered treaties, extinguished First Nations' titles to their land. That is reflected in the written texts of the treaties. Treaty 1 states that First Nations agreed to "cede, release, surrender and yield up to Her Majesty the Queen and successors forever all the lands included within the following limits." Canada, under British law, had purchased Rupert's Land from the Hudson's Bay Company a year earlier and considered it Dominion property. Treaties were seen by Ottawa, and still are, as agreements within that land ownership framework.

---

20 *Daily British Whig*, Kingston, Ontario, Oct. 5, 1871.

21 Elder David Courchene in an interview with the *Winnipeg Free Press*, June 21, 2021. Courchene was the founder of the Turtle Lodge International Centre for Indigenous Education and Wellness. He passed away on Dec. 8, 2021, not long after this interview.

However, that was not how First Nations viewed the treaties then—or now. Indigenous leaders were not consulted on the HBC land deal and did not approve it. They often complained to Indian commissioners during treaty negotiations that the land upon which their people had lived for thousands of years was sold without their consent. While they agreed to coexist with newcomers, there is little historical evidence—other than claims made by treaty commissioners—that First Nations explicitly agreed to the land surrender clauses in the treaties. "That was never in the mindset of our people that they were going to surrender all this land; they looked at it from the point of view of sharing," David Courchene said. First Nations knew their lands would be settled by newcomers and felt compelled to secure some type of agreement with the Crown to protect their territories and their way of life, he continued. "Whatever agreements that were signed, they saw that if they didn't do something, I think that they felt that they were going to be wiped right out."

Senior government officials, including Treaty 1 Indian commissioner Wemyss Simpson, claimed at the time that the Chiefs, through interpreters, agreed to cede their land. However, there are no records from independent sources to verify that claim. Nowhere in the detailed newspaper coverage from *The Manitoban* (which both Simpson and Lieutenant-Governor Adams Archibald accepted as an accurate account of the deliberations) were there reports of Chiefs agreeing to cede or surrender land. Discussions did take place around the exclusive use by settlers of limited tracts of lands that would become off-limits to First Nations. But there were also documented promises, reported in *The Manitoban*, made by Simpson and Archibald during negotiations that vast tracts of land would remain unoccupied where Indigenous people could continue to hunt, fish and trap as they always had.

"Till these lands are needed for use, you will be free to hunt over them, and make all the use of them which you have made in the past," Archibald said during talks. "But when lands are needed to be tilled or occupied, you must not go on them anymore. There will still be plenty of land that is neither tilled nor occupied, where you can go and roam and hunt as you have always done." If more land for First Nations was required in the future, Canada would set aside more territory for them, Archibald pledged. That promise was neither included in the text of the treaty nor in the so-called outside promises that were added to the treaty four years later. However, it was part of the verbal commitments made to First Nations, as recorded in *The Manitoban*.

Either way, it was made clear to First Nations they could continue to use vast tracts of land, including territory outside of their allotted reserves. They would not have to cede or surrender that territory. If they needed more reserve territory in the future as their communities grew, Canada would provide them with it, Archibald said. It's not difficult to see how First Nations walked away from treaty negotiations believing they would still have access to all the land they needed, and how that interpretation was passed down to subsequent generations through oral history.

First Nations' relationship with the land is not something that can be extinguished in a treaty, said Treaty 1 Elder Florence Paynter of Sandy Bay First Nation. "*Cede* is not even in the vocabulary of our people simply because we don't own the land. We were placed here by the creator and our stories that are passed on to us from one generation to the next has [*sic*] always upheld that we will share." Paynter further stated that her ancestors agreed to share the land with newcomers, not surrender or cede it, as settler governments claimed. "We come from two different mindsets: ownership and sharing are two totally different concepts. I think that's where the misunderstanding happened," she said. "Sure, we'll share the land with you but let us continue to be who we are as a people, to continue to hunt, trap and fish . . . If there [were] more of an understanding of what the treaties mean, I think people would be more open and [engaged in] respecting our people."[22]

What is clear is that the numbered treaties did not require Indigenous people to relinquish their sovereignty. Nowhere in the texts of the treaties does it stipulate that First Nations would become subordinate to the federal or provincial governments. Treaty commissioners often repeated

---

[22] Elder Florence Paynter interview, *Winnipeg Free Press*, June 28, 2021.

[23] The only exception to this would be the stipulation in the treaties that intoxicating substances would be banned on reserves.

during talks with First Nations leaders that the Crown would not interfere in the lives of Indigenous peoples.[23] They would help First Nations transition to an agriculture-based economy by providing them with farm implements when, or if, individual Indigenous communities chose to do so. The Crown would also provide schools on reserves for educational purposes, but only upon request by Indigenous communities. "Understand me, I do not want to interfere with your hunting and fishing," Alexander Morris, Manitoba's second lieutenant-governor and the chief negotiator for Treaties 3 through 6, told First Nations Chiefs during Treaty 4 talks in the Saskatchewan region. "I want you to pursue it through the country, as you have heretofore done."[24]

Morris encouraged the Chiefs to take up farming "to find food for themselves and their children that come after them," as government negotiators often did during treaty talks. "Sometimes when you go to hunt, you can leave your wives and children at home to take care of your gardens," said Morris.[25] However, taking up farming or abandoning traditional ways of life was never a condition of the numbered treaties, nor was giving up Indigenous rights to self-government. Chiefs were told they were "subjects of the Queen" and would have to obey the laws of the land. But they never agreed, nor were they asked, to give up their way of life.

Morris made similar statements during Treaty 3 negotiations in northwestern Ontario, telling First Nations leaders they would be able to continue to hunt and fish on lands outside their allotted reserves for an indeterminate amount of time. "It may be a long time before the other lands are wanted, and in the meantime, you will be permitted to fish and hunt over them."[26]

That is a crucial point passed down through Indigenous oral history. "Your ancestors and my ancestors went into an agreement that they would not interfere with anything that our people were doing," Paynter explained, "with the understanding that our people would be free to live. The treaties

---

[24] Morris, *Treaties of Canada*, 204.

[25] Morris, 204.

[26] Treaty 3 negotiations, Oct. 1, 1873, in Morris, *Treaties of Canada*, 58.

were made on trust, respect, and they were based on a handshake. They were based on the promise that we would live side by side and we would continue to be who we are in our own spaces."[27]

Historical records show many of the oral promises made during treaty talks were not included in the written text. Some of the commitments made during Treaty 1 negotiations, but not included in the text—which Ottawa called the "outside promises"—were added to the treaty four years after it was signed, including the supply of farm implements to First Nations. The inclusion of those promises only occurred after several years of persistent lobbying by First Nations. Some Chiefs protested by refusing to accept their annuities until matters were resolved.

Federal negotiators had underestimated, or had little knowledge of, the extent to which First Nations could recall, months or years later, verbal commitments made during treaty negotiations. They were often shocked when communities, through their knowledge keepers, could recite verbatim promises made during conferences. That proved problematic for the federal government when First Nations later came to them and demanded to know why certain promises made during negotiations had not been fulfilled. Simpson and Archibald were under tremendous pressure to finalize an agreement and may have made promises through interpreters they knew they could not keep. Had they done so in desperation to conclude a deal, during the final days of talks, when it appeared that First Nations negotiators might walk away? If they had, they had underestimated the negotiating skills of their treaty partners. Whatever the case, it prompted Archibald to issue a warning to Ottawa on the importance of fulfilling its treaty commitments.

"It is impossible to be too particular in carrying out the terms of the arrangements made with these people," wrote Adams Archibald, several months after negotiating Treaties 1 and 2. "They recollect with astonishing accuracy every stipulation made at the treaty, and if we expect our relations with them to be of the kind which it is desirable to maintain, we must fulfil our obligations with scrupulous fidelity."[28]

---

[27] Paynter interview, *Winnipeg Free Press*, June 28, 2021.

Simon J. Dawson, a civil engineer in charge of constructing a road between Lake Superior and Lake of the Woods in the late 1860s and early 1870s, remarked in a report to Parliament how First Nations representatives could accurately recall, sometimes years later, conversations with government officials. Dawson, who served as an Indian commissioner during Treaty 3 talks, described Saulteaux Chiefs in the Lake of the Woods region as "very intelligent" and "extremely jealous as to their right of soil and authority over the country which they occupy."[29] But when they made a commitment to government officials, Dawson wrote, they honoured it.

> At these gatherings it is necessary to observe extreme caution in what is said, as, though they have no means of writing, there are always those present, who are charged to keep every word in mind. As an instance of the manner in which the records are in this way kept, without writing, I may mention that, on one occasion, at Fort Frances, the principal Chief of the tribe commenced an oration, by repeating, almost verbatim, what I had said to him two years previously.
>
> All this goes to show a certain stability of character, and a degree of importance attached to what they say, on such occasions, themselves, as well as to what they hear from others. The word of the Chiefs once passed, too, seems to be quite reliable, and this augurs well for the observance of any treaty that may be made with them.[30]

When the federal government agreed in 1875 to add some of the oral promises to Treaty 1, they described the omissions as a "misunderstanding," even though Ottawa knew immediately following treaty talks that some of the verbal commitments made had been excluded from the text. That was confirmed by federal Minister of the Interior David Laird in a report to Parliament in 1876:

---

[28] Letter from Adams Archibald to Governor General John Young, Feb. 12, 1872, House of Commons sessional papers, 1873, vol. 5, no. 23, 1.

[29] Report to Parliament by Simon J. Dawson, Apr. 20, 1868, House of Commons sessional papers, 1867–68, vol. 9, no. 81, 27.

[30] Dawson, Apr. 20, 1868, 28.

> This unfortunate controversy between the Government and the Indians originated in certain verbal promises, made by the Commissioners, at the time of negotiating treaties Nos. 1 and 2—promises which were neither embodied in the text of these Treaties, nor in any way recognized, or referred to, when those Treaties were ratified in September, 1871. On a careful examination of the papers connected with the subject, it was found that a memorandum was appended to the original Treaty No. 1, signed by Mr. Commissioner Simpson, His Honour Governor Archibald, Mr. St. John, and the Hon. Mr. McKay, purporting to contain their understanding of the terms upon which the Indians concluded the Treaty. (A copy of this memorandum is appended to this report.) It further appeared, that although this memorandum was not formally sanctioned when the Treaties were ratified, the validity of the promises therein made, was admitted by the then Superintendent General of Indian Affairs, and repeatedly referred to, and at least partially recognized, in official despatches from their Honors Lieut.-Governors Archibald and Morris, as well as in the reports of the Indian Commissioner, and in the minutes of the North-West Council.[31]

Molyneux St. John, an Indian agent who took part in the Treaty 1 talks (whom Laird refers to in his report), provided a lengthy written account of how verbal commitments were made during negotiations but were omitted from the final text. He said many pledges were made, including by Archibald, that First Nations leaders accepted as binding but that were later excluded.

According to St. John, the memorandum attached to the treaty was written almost immediately after the conclusion of the negotiations:

> The proceedings were over but a short time before it became evident that there was some misunderstanding, and with the view of setting the matter at rest, as far as regarded one side, His Excellency the then

[31] Report to Parliament by Minister of the Interior David Laird, Jan. 31, 1876, House of Commons sessional papers, 1876, vol. 7, no. 9, vi.

> Lieutenant-Governor, asked Mr. Commissioner Simpson, the Hon. James McKay and myself, as the persons knowing best the circumstances and details of the matter, to join with him in signing a list of articles which we severally and collectively understood to be the things promised to the Indians but not mentioned in the Treaty. Some little discussion took place about this, but it was eventually signed, and, I believe, forwarded to Ottawa with the Treaty, in October, 1871.[32]

The memorandum was not an exhaustive list of excluded promises. It was limited to commitments made that St. John, McKay, Archibald and Simpson could collectively recall and agree on. It "by no means" covered everything the Chiefs understood was part of the agreement, wrote St. John. There were other promises made that were not included in either the written text or the memorandum. Those exclusions, and the failure to make good on many of the promises made—such as immediately setting aside reserve land for First Nations—soured relations between First Nations and the federal government. The "untrustworthy nature" of Archibald and Simpson's promises was "thrown in our teeth," every time Indian Affairs officials subsequently met with First Nations, wrote St. John.

> There is no difference of sentiment amongst them [First Nations] on this point; however remote they may be from one another, their demands and assertions are alike. In every case the cry has been the same, and there is not a shadow of a doubt that when they left the Grand Council at the Stone Fort they were firmly impressed with the idea that the demands which they had made had been, with few exceptions, granted by the Queen's representatives.[33]

Archibald was a key negotiator during the talks. Whether he had the authority to make the commitments he did on behalf of the commissioner was immaterial to First Nations. As far as they understood it, Archibald

[32] Letter written by Molyneux St. John to federal government, Feb. 24, 1873, House of Commons sessional papers, 1873, vol. 5, no. 23, 12.

[33] St. John to federal government, Feb. 24, 1873, 12.

was speaking on behalf of the Queen and his words were binding. "I am not aware whether or not Mr. Archibald was a joint Commissioner with Mr. Simpson, but he was the central figure at the Council table, and the Indians attached as much weight to his utterances as to those of Mr. Commissioner Simpson," wrote St. John.[34]

It was not just farm implements that had been promised but were excluded from the text of the treaty. The Chiefs had also been promised that government would send farmers to reserves to teach them to cultivate the land and provide them with blacksmiths and carpenters to help build the infrastructure needed for farming. They were also promised clothing for themselves and their families, and food when they required it in the winter, according to St. John. He wrote: "As most, if not all, of these things were spoken of during the negotiations of the Treaty, and as the Indians never understood the line of assent and dissent of the Commissioner, the latter has given, in those cases where he deemed it expedient, such articles as he thought would really benefit the Indians."[35] The rest was excluded, at the discretion of the commissioner. "The full demands of the Indians cannot of course be complied with, but there is nevertheless a certain paradox in asking a wild Indian, who has hitherto gained his livelihood by hunting and trapping, to settle down on a reservation and cultivate the land without, at the same time, offering him some means of making his living," wrote St. John.[36]

The so-called outside promises may have existed outside the written text of the treaty, but they were not peripheral to the negotiations between the Crown and First Nations. They were no less important than those that ended up in the written version. Morris referred to them as "unrecorded" promises. However, the commitments were recorded in the memorandum that was attached to the written text of the treaty. In many cases they were specific verbal pledges made by government negotiators but were, inexplicably or conveniently, excluded from the written text. The provision for

[34] St. John to federal government, Feb. 24, 1873, 12.

[35] St. John to federal government, Feb. 24, 1873, 13.

[36] St. John to federal government, Feb. 24, 1873, 14.

farm implements, for example, was raised by Henry Prince, the Chief of the St. Peter's band, during negotiations when he asked how First Nations were supposed to farm without equipment and supplies. The discussions around that, and the ultimate commitment by federal negotiators to provide those supplies, did not occur outside of official talks; they were part of the negotiations.

The omissions and the acknowledgement by Ottawa that Indian commissioners had overstepped their boundaries when making some of those promises was reported publicly after both sides agreed in 1875 to include the outside promises in Treaty 1. The *Daily Free Press* in Winnipeg reported on David Laird's 1876 report to Parliament: "Mr. Laird says the controversy with Manitoba Indians, in connexion with the so-called outside promises, has been adjusted in a manner satisfactory alike to the Government and to the Indians. These claims arose from the Indian Commissioners having exceeded their powers."[37]

First Nations had agreed to share the land with newcomers as long as the Crown lived up to its obligations. When government immediately reneged on some of those commitments by excluding certain promises from the text of the treaty, the honour of the Crown was compromised in the eyes of First Nations. Why those promises were not added to the treaty's text, which was written by government officials, was never adequately explained by treaty commissioners.

Although some of the verbal commitments were added in 1875 through negotiations with First Nations, not all of them made it into the written text. Ottawa did not agree to all the demands made by the Chiefs. There were disagreements in some cases over what had been promised. When Alexander Morris and treaty commissioner James McKay negotiated the inclusion of outside promises with Chief Yellow Quill from the Portage band, Morris described the Chief as uncooperative. "This band has always been troublesome," wrote Morris.[38] However, Yellow Quill had a legitimate grievance. During Treaty 1 talks, the Portage band was promised reserve

[37] *Daily Free Press*, Winnipeg, Manitoba, Mar. 17, 1876.

[38] Morris, *Treaties of Canada*, 128.

land on both sides of the Assiniboine River, a pledge that McKay, the interpreter for the Crown during those negotiations, confirmed. It was another example of a verbal promise made that was not included in the original 1871 text. A compromise was eventually reached, but Yellow Quill's demands were never fully met.

As part of the updates to Treaties 1 and 2 in 1875, the federal government also raised the annuity to $5 per person from $3 "out of good feeling to the Indians and as a matter of benevolence." The increase matched the $5 annuities that were negotiated in Treaty 3 in 1873. In exchange, First Nations agreed to abandon all future claims to verbal promises made during Treaty 1 and 2 talks, other than those included in the updated written text.

TREATIES 2 THROUGH 5

Treaty 2 was negotiated almost immediately after Treaty 1 at Manitoba Post, and its terms were virtually identical to those of Treaty 1. Negotiations took only a few days to complete. Treaties 1 and 2 were often referred to together in the late nineteenth century, almost as though they were one treaty.

Treaty 2 was concluded on August 21, 1871. It was an important agreement for the federal government as it opened up a vast territory west of Treaty 1 for colonial settlement. A small portion of Treaty 2 spills into present-day Saskatchewan, but the bulk of it is in present-day central Manitoba. It would be the second of eleven numbered treaties negotiated between the Crown and First Nations in northwestern Ontario and western Canada.

There are no newspaper or other transcripts of Treaty 2 negotiations. *The Manitoban* ran only a single paragraph following the signing of the treaty: "This extinguishes the Indian title held over a large and beautiful tract of the North-West and with the treaty recently made for the Province, opens a most important sector of territory for colonization."[39] The newspaper report, although brief, underscored the common Euro-Canadian interpretation of treaties at the time: that they were instruments to clear

[39] *The Manitoban*, Aug. 26, 1871. The treaty recently made for Manitoba refers to Treaty 1.

the way for non-Indigenous settlement by "extinguish[ing] the Indian title." Even though treaties were presented to First Nations as bilateral agreements designed to achieve peaceful coexistence, they were often seen by non-Indigenous Canadians and governments as land acquisition deals. The federal Department of the Interior, which had responsibility for Indian Affairs in the mid-1870s, described First Nations people as more of an administrative burden than as partners and cohabitants of the land. "The enormous extension of the area of the Dominion within the last few years has necessarily added proportionately to the work thrown upon the staff of the Geological Survey, while the accession of some 55,000 red men, for the most part utterly uncivilized, has added still more seriously to the labors and responsibilities of the Indian Branch," the department wrote.[40]

After several failed attempts by Canada in 1871 and 1872 to negotiate a treaty with First Nations in northwestern Ontario, Treaty 3 was signed in 1873, a small portion of which extends into Manitoba. Alexander Morris, who took over from Adams Archibald as lieutenant-governor of Manitoba and the North-West Territories in 1872, was the chief negotiator for the Crown. He also led negotiations at Fort Qu'Appelle in the Saskatchewan region, where First Nations signed Treaty 4 in 1874. Treaty 5, the fifth numbered treaty in present-day Manitoba, was negotiated and signed in 1875, with amendments made the following year to include additional Indigenous communities. Several adhesions were made to Treaty 5 up until 1910 to include First Nations farther north. While most of Treaty 5 is in present-day Manitoba, some of it extends into present-day Northwestern Ontario and Saskatchewan.

Unlike previous numbered treaties, Treaty 5 was not negotiated in a single location. Commissioners Alexander Morris and James McKay travelled on the HBC steamship the *Colville* for nearly two weeks, covering some thousand miles around Lake Winnipeg to several First Nations, including at Berens River, Norway House and the mouth of the Saskatchewan River. McKay, an English-speaking Métis from Red River who was fluent in Cree,

---

40 Report to Parliament by Minister of the Interior David Laird, Jan. 20, 1875, House of Commons sessional papers, 1875, vol. 7, no. 8, 2–3.

was employed by the federal government to act as interpreter during several treaty negotiations and was a commissioner for Treaty 5 talks. McKay, who Morris described as a "remarkable man," was hired for his language skills and his knowledge of Indigenous people, although mainly to advance the interests of the federal government, not First Nations. McKay had been instrumental in bringing the two sides together during the final day of Treaty 1 negotiations in 1871 and later served as speaker of Manitoba's legislative council. "Thoroughly understanding the Indian character, he possessed large influence over the Indian tribes, which he always used for the benefit and the advantage of the government," wrote Morris.[41]

Several more Indigenous communities were added to Treaty 5 the following year when commissioners Thomas Howard and Lestock Reid travelled by sailboat to communities in the north. In all, Treaty 5 comprised forty First Nations.

The federal government was eager to negotiate Treaty 5, in large part to secure access to Lake Winnipeg and the rivers that drain into and out of the massive body of water. Soon after Manitoba joined Canada, federal officials realized how rich the region was in natural resources and how important it was to secure transportation routes in the area for economic growth. Reserves for First Nations in Treaty 5 were often chosen by treaty commissioners to maximize settler access to rivers and lakes. Little consideration was given to the future livelihoods of First Nations. Some Indigenous communities were paid to relocate to accommodate the economic and trade interests of newcomers. The primary goal of the treaty commissioners was to clear the way for settlers to capitalize on the region's valuable natural resources. Morris reported on the richness of the territory to Minister of the Interior David Laird in glowing terms: "I may mention here that the prevalence of timber suitable for fuel and building purposes, of lime and sandstone, of much good soil, and natural hay lands on the west shore of the lake, together with great abundance of white fish, sturgeon and other fish in the lake, will ensure, ere long, a large settlement."[42]

---

[41] Morris, *Treaties of Canada*, 144.

[42] Letter from Alexander Morris to David Laird, Nov. 17, 1876, in Morris, *Treaties of Canada*, 150.

The same year, Laird reported to Parliament the importance of negotiating treaties with First Nations around Lake Winnipeg to gain access to the area's rich natural resources:

> On the west side of the lake the soil in some localities is admirable for agricultural purposes and the country is in every way adapted for early settlement. Moreover, pending the construction of the portion of the pacific Railway lying west of Lake Winnipeg, the Lake and the Saskatchewan river are destined to become the principal thoroughfare of communication between Manitoba and the fertile prairies in the West. For these reasons it was essential that the Indian title to all territory in the vicinity of the Lake should be extinguished, so that settlers and traders might have undisturbed access to its waters, shores, islands, inlets and tributary streams. The mouth of the Saskatchewan river especially seems to be of importance as presenting an eligible site for a future town. All these considerations pointed to the necessity of prompt negotiation with the Indians on both sides of Lake Winnipeg for the surrender of their territory.[43]

Treaty 5 First Nations received considerably less for the settlement of their lands than the signatories of Treaties 3 and 4. The latter received 640 acres (1 square mile) of reserve land per family of five for their exclusive use. That was a significant increase from the 160 acres per family that First Nations received in Treaties 1 and 2.

Indigenous Chiefs demanded and received greater compensation during Treaty 3 negotiations in Northwestern Ontario after several years of failed negotiations. Crown officials, eager to conclude an agreement, were forced to sweeten the pot. That carried over to Treaty 4 in present-day Saskatchewan, where Chiefs also demanded and received greater compensation.

However, those land grants were reduced during Treaty 5 negotiations. Crown officials scaled back the reserve allocation to 160 acres per family of five, the same as in Treaty 1. Also, the one-time gratuity of $12 paid to each

---

[43] Laird, Jan. 31, 1876, viii.

First Nations person in Treaties 3 and 4 (more for Chiefs and councillors) was reduced to $5 for Treaty 5. The only compensation that remained the same was the $5 annuity for individuals.

It is not fully clear why compensation and land grants were scaled back for Treaty 5 First Nations. It may have been driven in part by political pressure in Ottawa to cut spending in Indian Affairs. By the mid-1870s, the growing costs of administering treaties were hotly debated in the House of Commons. Money spent providing First Nations with farm implements and other supplies was increasingly scrutinized. Many MPs demanded to know what value the government was getting for the expenditures. It's not surprising under those circumstances that treaty commissioners sought to reduce compensation and land allotments for First Nations.

The federal government was also concerned that allocating too much reserve land to First Nations would leave less valuable land for non-Indigenous settlers. As early as 1873 following the signing of Treaty 3, where treaty land allotments were substantially increased compared with Treaties 1 and 2, federal officials began discussing the prospect of reducing land allotments in future treaty negotiations.

J.A.N. Provencher, the Indian commissioner in Manitoba in 1873, urged Ottawa to consider shrinking reserve allotments for First Nations in future treaty negotiations. "If we grant a considerable extent, a square mile for instance to each family, as is mentioned in Treaty No. 3, as each family will be able to demand a lot of equal value, it will follow that these claims will comprise all the most desirable properties, and will render impossible whatever intentions the Government may have in paying the Indians for the relinquishment of their rights," he wrote.[44]

It is interesting that Provencher used the words "relinquishment of their rights." In fact, there is no documented evidence that First Nations agreed to relinquish their sovereignty or any of their other rights during treaty negotiations, including the right to maintain their culture, languages and way of living. They agreed to share land with newcomers and to accept al-

---

[44] Report to Parliament by Commissioner of Indian Affairs J.A.N. Provencher, Dec. 31, 1873, House of Commons sessional papers, 1875, vol. 7, no. 8, 55.

lotted reserves for their exclusive use, while still having access to territory outside of those reserves to hunt, fish and trap. They also agreed to accept annuities and other resources from the Crown to help compensate for the disruption caused by colonial settlement. Successive Indian commissioners made solemn pledges to First Nations that they would be able to maintain their sovereign and other rights.

To make things even more difficult for First Nations, it was easier for Indian commissioners to reduce compensation during Treaty 5 talks since many of the nations negotiated individually or in small groups. They did not have the same leverage as First Nations in previous treaty talks, where bargaining was done collectively on behalf of a larger number of communities.

Morris claimed First Nations received less compensation in Treaty 5 because fewer settlers would occupy the region compared with other parts of the country. However, commissioners Thomas Howard and Lestock Reid, who led negotiations farther north in 1876, told Indigenous Chiefs their compensation was reduced because land in northern Manitoba was less valuable than in Treaty 4 territory. "I at last made them understand the difference between their position and the Plain Indians,[45] by pointing out that the land they would surrender would be useless to the Queen, while what the Plain Indians gave up would be of value to her for homes for her white children," wrote Howard.[46] In the eyes of the commissioners, the value of the land was not measured by what it was worth to First Nations. Rather, it was based on how many homes it could provide for the Queen's "white children." The federal government's primary interest was in obtaining territorial access for white settlers at the expense of First Nations, who were marginalized in the process.

The racialization of treaty negotiations aside, the commissioner's position that the land was "useless" was clearly inaccurate and used solely as a bargaining tactic, since both Morris and Laird had confirmed that the

---

45 Howard and Reid told Chiefs in Treaty 5 that their land was less valuable than that of the Plains Indians in Treaty 4, which was why they were receiving less compensation.

46 Letter from Thomas Howard to Alexander Morris, Oct. 10, 1876, in Morris, *Treaties of Canada*, 162.

territory around Lake Winnipeg was rich with natural resources and of great value to the Crown. It is unlikely that Parliament would have paid compensation to settle the territory if the land were useless to the government, especially considering Ottawa's strained financial circumstances in the 1870s. Settlement around Lake Winnipeg was an important part of Canada's foray into the west, especially for Scandinavian settlers who had already established communities around the lake by that time. It is more likely the commissioners were simply looking to settle the territory at the lowest cost possible.

Like all the treaties, the written text of Treaty 5 claims First Nations ceded their territory and extinguished the title to their lands. However, as was the case for Treaty 2, there are no transcripts of Treaty 5 negotiations, only the one-sided letters and reports written by government officials. The shorthand notes taken by government officials during Treaty 3 and 4 negotiations (and published by Morris) were also written from Ottawa's perspective. However, similar to the detailed newspaper coverage in *The Manitoban* for Treaty 1, the transcripts provide valuable insight into the conflicts and disagreements that arose during talks. They include some of the commitments made by commissioners that were not included in the text of the treaties and reveal the anger and frustration of First Nations over the unilateral sale of their homeland from HBC to Canada. Because no independent evidence, transcripts or third-party accounts exist of what transpired during Treaty 5 talks, there is even greater doubt around claims by Indian commissioners that, in Treaty 5, First Nations agreed to surrender their territory.

Shorthand notes and newspaper accounts of negotiations for Treaties 1, 3 and 4 are important because they also reveal some of the bargaining strategies and intimidation tactics employed by commissioners during negotiations. There is no reason to believe that those same tactics were not used during negotiations for Treaties 2 and 5. Morris, for example, told First Nations Chiefs during Treaty 4 negotiations that Queen Victoria did not believe the Royal Charter granted to HBC in 1670 was fair. He claimed the Queen wanted to alter the arrangement. "Many, many years ago, before we were born, one of the kings gave the company certain rights to trade in this country," he said. The Queen did not think what her "father's father" had done was "just," and she wanted equality for all instead, Morris explained. "Therefore, she told the company that the time had come when they should no longer be the great power in this country. The Queen then told the company that she would govern the country herself, and she told them she would give them some land."[47] The Queen would also ensure First Nations received their share of land, Morris told the Chiefs.

Morris's strategy was to present the Queen as a benevolent ruler who had First Nations' best interests at heart, even though treaty offers were often presented as ultimatums by commissioners. When impasses were reached during negotiations, Morris—on behalf of the Crown—and Indian commissioner Simpson before him, would often threaten that if they could not reach a deal, the offers on the table would disappear for good and First Nations would be left with nothing. Those actions, carried out by representatives of the Queen, were hardly the actions of a benevolent ruler.

Treaty 3 negotiations were recorded in shorthand by an unnamed soldier of the militia, which Morris reprinted in his book, *The Treaties of Canada with the Indians of Manitoba and the North-West Territories*. Morris wrote that the shorthand notes "present an accurate view of the course of the discussions, and a vivid representation of the habits of Indian thought."[48]

The transcript reveals some of the struggles and disagreements that took place between Treaty 3 Chiefs and Morris, including how the commissioner threatened them with ultimatums when he thought their demands were too high. Chief Ma-We-Do-Pe-Nais, the leading spokesman for the Saulteaux First Nations, demanded twice as much as Morris was offering. He also complained that settlers had already begun occupying First Nations land. "It is our chiefs, our young men, our children and great-grand children, and those that are to be born, that I represent here, and it is for them I ask for terms," Ma-We-Do-Pe-Nais told Morris through his interpreter. "The white man has robbed us of our riches, and we don't wish to give them up again without getting something in their place."

Morris replied that his offer was fair and liberal, and he was prepared to

---

[47] Morris, *Treaties of Canada*, 103.

[48] Morris, *Treaties of Canada*, 52.

walk away if the Chiefs did not accept it. "For your children, grand-children, and children unborn, I am sorry that you will not accept of my terms. I shall go home sorry, but it is your own doing; I must simply go back and report the fact that you refuse to make a treaty with me."[49] The transcripts also show how Morris used divisive tactics to pit nations against each other by suggesting he could sign treaties with some individually and not others.

Much like Treaty 1 negotiations, some of the verbal promises made during Treaty 3 talks were not included in the text of the agreement but were reported in the shorthand accounts by the unknown soldier. Among them was a pledge by the commissioner that First Nations would be exempt from military conscription. Another was that First Nations would be compensated for minerals found on their lands. Neither were included in the text of the treaty.

Without shorthand transcripts or newspaper reports of Treaty 5 talks, less is known about the dialogue that occurred between First Nations and Crown officials. Correspondence and reports written by government officials describe Treaty 5 negotiations as amicable and "successful." They also claim First Nations agreed to all land surrender clauses.

Minister of the Interior David Laird reflected that when he reported to Parliament in 1876 on Treaty 5 negotiations: "The cordial welcome everywhere extended by the Indians to the Commissioners, the readiness with which they accepted the terms offered, and their gratitude to the Government of the Dominion for its liberality in dealing with them, are gratifying evidences of the good feeling generally existing at present among the Indians in this portion of the Territories."[50]

Treaty 5 Elders have a different interpretation of what occurred during negotiations. They say the oral history passed down through generations states unequivocally that land was not surrendered and that their sovereignty and inherent rights were never relinquished. The *Treaty 5 Okimaawin Reference Guide* states the following about land surrenders:

---

49 Morris, *Treaties of Canada*, 62.

50 Laird, Jan. 31, 1876, x.

> No reasonable person should believe or be made to believe our ancestors consented to extinguishing the vast territories of our people. That is nonsense. The words *cede* and *surrender* have no conceptual meaning in our language or culture and are contrary to our worldview . . . that the Creator held all lands and land is sacrosanct. It cannot be given up at the whim of the settler. Creator law does not sanction this type of transfer in land. We are the land. The common treaty understanding by our people is that land and resources are to be shared. That was the agreement and our understanding with the settler society, and we would continue with our avocations and continue to use our natural resources for sustenance and to sustain our governments.[51]

The inherent rights of First Nations to continue with those avocations and to preserve their culture and language were under attack by the federal government almost immediately after the earliest numbered treaties were signed. One of the most important commitments made by the Crown during treaty talks—that Indigenous people would not be forced to relinquish their way of life, or "live like the white man" against their will—was betrayed. Five years after Treaty 1 was negotiated, and a year after the first Treaty 5 agreements were concluded, Ottawa passed the Indian Act. While the legislation was originally meant to consolidate the various laws that governed Indigenous peoples, the act was the beginning of Ottawa's persistent and explicit attempts to control Indigenous people and assimilate them into Euro-Canadian Christian society.

David Laird, minister of the interior in 1876, wrote in the months leading up to the introduction of the Indian Act in Parliament that the proposed legislation would lift First Nations out of their "condition of tutelage and dependence." He said First Nations had until then been treated as wards of the state and needed to be prepared for "higher civilization" through "education and every other means."[52]

---

[51] Summit of Treaty 5 Sovereign Nations, "Preface," in *Treaty 5 Okimaawin Reference Guide*, May 2020, xv.

[52] Laird, Jan. 31, 1876, xiii.

J.A.N. Provencher underscored that belief in a report to Parliament when he described First Nations as ignorant and uncivilized. They would become beggars if they did not adopt the ways of the white man, he wrote.

> There are two modes wherein the Government may treat the Indian nations who inhabit this territory. Treaties may be made with them simply with a view to the extinction of their rights, by agreeing to pay them a sum, and afterwards abandon them to themselves. On the other side, they may be instructed, civilized and led to a mode of life more in conformity with the new position of this country, and accordingly make them good, industrious and useful citizens. Under the first system the Indians will remain in their condition of ignorance and inferiority, and as soon as the facilities for hunting and fishing disappear, they will become mendicants, or be obliged to seek refuge in localities inaccessible to immigration or cultivation. Under the second system, on the contrary, they will learn sufficient for themselves, and to enable them to pass from a state of tutelage, and to do without assistance from the Government. The best means to break them of their roving habits, to elevate and assure their position, is to attach them to agriculture.[53]

Provencher wrote in an 1875 report that it was only by abandoning their culture and way of life—including "forgetting their native tongue"—that First Nations could become productive members of Canadian society.

> All those who have taken an interest in the future welfare of the Indians have directed their minds to their education, and have insisted on the necessity of raising the level of their knowledge, of enlightening their minds, and above all of acting early on the minds of the children, so as to give them at an age when they are more susceptible of receiving an impression, intellectual habits, which are the most striking feature of civilization. The necessity of having the

[53] Provencher, Dec. 31, 1873, 56.

> Indians forget their native tongue has been urged several times, and under many circumstances, and it was believed that if it ever could be accomplished, it would be the main step taken towards their advancement . . .[54]

It was not only government officials who viewed Indigenous people as an inferior race of people. According to William Spragge, deputy superintendent of Indian Affairs in 1874, anti-Indigenous views existed broadly in Canadian society. He wrote that attempts to push First Nations off their reserves, despite the legal provisions of the treaties, were commonplace. Almost three years after the signing of Treaty 1, Indigenous people were facing increasing marginalization. They were being systematically displaced.

> The fact cannot be disguised that in too many quarters an intolerance of Indians as a race is continually manifested, and the limited number of acres which a humane care of them demands, are begrudged them; and efforts to effect their removal from the reserves guaranteed them by solemn treaty and contract are not infrequent. The knowledge which reaches them of attempts made to transfer them from their reserves to remoter localities, is to them both harassing and prejudicial. Fortunately, they are protected by statute. But they are not unaware that law does not always remain the same . . . The claims of the Indians to liberal consideration, as respects their condition and their rights, and the obligation to promote their welfare, has now-a-days few advocates, and not a year passes but that attempts are made to acquire from them the little remnants of reserved lands which they occupy.[55]

The deputy superintendent's observations were in stark contrast to statements made by Joseph Howe, secretary of state for the provinces in the

[54] Report to Parliament by Commissioner of Indian Affairs J.A.N. Provencher, Oct. 30, 1875, House of Commons sessional papers, 1876, vol. 7, no. 9, 35.

[55] Letter written by Deputy Superintendent of Indian Affairs William Spragge, March 18, 1874, annual report for the year ending June 30, 1874, House of Commons sessional papers, 1874, vol. 6, no. 17, 5–6.

early 1870s, who claimed Canada had a stellar record in the treatment of Indigenous people. Spragge confirmed in his report that "few advocates" in Canada were prepared to advance the rights and welfare of Indigenous people. And even when they believed they were acting in the best interests of Indigenous people, they did so through a paternalistic lens of cultural and racial superiority. The policy goals—whether pursued by Indian agents, Indian commissioners or politicians—rarely, if ever, included co-existing with Indigenous communities as equal partners in an environment of cultural parity and mutual respect. Colonial governments did not value Indigenous culture and way of life, including their spiritual connection to the land. Consequently, the only path to "progress" and "civilization" in their eyes was to convince, and eventually coerce, Indigenous people to adopt the white man's way of living in an agriculture-based economy.

Indian agent Molyneux St. John predicted First Nations would perish if they did not abandon their traditional way of life and settle down on reserves to farm. St. John wrote that the federal government could either provide First Nations with annuities and allow them to continue living their lives as they had before, including fishing, hunting and trapping, or induce them to settle down on reserves and abandon their traditional way of life. He offered predictions for both scenarios: "In the former case all the promises real and alleged could be commuted for a sum of money down, and the Indians would gradually disappear from here to re-appear in diminished numbers farther west; but taking the latter view as the more desirable one, the necessity of helping the Indian rather with what he really requires than with what he thinks he wants, seems to me to be beyond a doubt."[56]

Federal officials showed little interest in embracing Indigenous culture or in exploring ways of living together in harmony with the original inhabitants of the land. That was in contrast to pre-Confederation years, when European settlers and traders often maintained mutually respectful and mutually beneficial relations with Indigenous people and relied on them and their way of life to help them survive and to navigate the land. They often intermarried and shared in each other's cultural celebrations, habits

---

[56] St. John, Feb. 24, 1873, 14.

and dress. That level of respect largely evaporated once settlement in the west began in earnest.

Joseph Howe, whose idea of the proper treatment of Indigenous people was to assimilate them into white culture, remarked in 1873 that eastern Canada had examples of how Indigenous people could blend in with the "higher class" of white culture once they were sufficiently educated and had abandoned their traditional modes of life. "In the Canadas it is not a rare thing to meet Indian gentlemen as well educated, as well dressed, as careful in their habits, and as courteous in their manners as are the higher class of white men to be found in our rural districts, or even in our cities," he wrote.[57]

Property ownership and the accumulation of material wealth, while valued in European culture, was foreign to Indigenous culture. The reluctance of colonial governments to accept that fact and instead impose their values on another culture was the driving force behind the Indian Act. Indigenous culture, language and spirituality was seen by colonial governments as a curse inherited from past generations that needed to be expunged.

David Laird, minister of the interior in 1875, summed up that colonial mentality in an Indian Affairs report to Parliament under the heading of "Individual Property":

> It is gratifying to observe that the Indians on several of the reserves are beginning to acquire individual property. They are making small clearances on their allotments, raising patches of grain and vegetables and procuring farm stock.
>
> But the progress is slow. Habits formed by a people generations back are difficult to overcome. The system of living with the rude savage is from hand to mouth. He has no inducement to acquire property, because it would only further expose him to the attacks of his enemies. He is active on the war-path or in the chase; but when danger is over, revenge satisfied, or his immediate wants appeased, he

[57] Indian Affairs annual report for year ending June 30, 1872, House of Commons sessional papers, 1873, vol. 5, no. 23, 2.

> relapses into his accustomed indolence. It may be said that this inertia is the chief legacy which he bequeaths to his children.
>
> The great difficulty with the Indian is that he cannot all at once rid himself of this inheritance. Even under the most favourable circumstances time must be given him to understand the motives and acquire the habits of the white man, who labors to accumulate wealth in order that he may have the means of support in sickness or old age, or of giving his offspring a start in life.
>
> But when these motives come to be understood and acted upon by the Indian, the evidence of which is the possession of considerable property acquired by his own industry and thrift, it shows that he may safely be entrusted with the rights of full citizenship. To grant enfranchisement to the intelligent and well-behaved Indians would probably train them to still further self-reliance, and encourage their brethren who are lagging behind to make greater exertions to overtake the Anglo-Saxon in the race of progress.[58]

When efforts to convince Indigenous people to abandon their culture and way of life largely failed, governments and the churches began using force through aggressive assimilative policies under the Indian Act, including mandatory attendance at residential schools and the banning of Indigenous language and cultural rituals. The deep damage and tragic consequences that ensued caused generations of trauma within Indigenous communities. It was not until 2008 that the prime minister of Canada officially apologized for government's role in those genocidal policies:

> Two primary objectives of the residential schools system were to remove and isolate children from the influence of their homes, families, traditions and cultures, and to assimilate them into the dominant culture. These objectives were based on the assumption Aboriginal cultures and spiritual beliefs were inferior and unequal. Indeed, some sought, as it was infamously said, "to kill the Indian in the child."

---

[58] Report to Parliament by Minister of the Interior David Laird, Jan. 20, 1875, House of Commons sessional papers, 1875, vol. 7, no. 8, 5–6.

> Today, we recognize that this policy of assimilation was wrong, has caused great harm, and has no place in our country.[59]

Pope Francis observed fourteen years later, during a historic visit to Canada when he apologized for the Catholic Church's involvement in residential schools, that European settlers had missed an opportunity to embrace Indigenous culture and to live in harmony with those who first inhabited the land. "When the European colonists first arrived here, there was a great opportunity to bring about a fruitful encounter between cultures, traditions and forms of spirituality," he said. "Yet, for the most part, that did not happen." Pope Francis described attempts by the church and governments to extinguish Indigenous culture and language as "evil" and a "disastrous error" that was incompatible with the Gospel of Jesus Christ. "It is painful to think of how the firm soil of values, language and culture that made up the authentic identity of your peoples was eroded, and that you have continued to pay the price of this," he told the assembled crowd of Indigenous people.[60]

Colonialism grew rapidly in the west in the 1870s following the signing of the first numbered treaties. Thousands of settlers a year from eastern Canada poured into Manitoba to take advantage of government land grants and to seize the agricultural and trade opportunities the treaties opened up. Regardless of the contrasting perspectives of First Nations and the federal government on the meaning, interpretation and purpose of the numbered treaties, they became part of the legal framework of Manitoba. That was well understood in eastern Canada, which saw the signing of the treaties as the key to settling the west.

The *Kingston Daily News* in Ontario reported shortly after the signing of Treaty 2 that Manitoba was now ripe for settlement:

---

[59] Prime Minister Stephen Harper's official apology for Canada's use of residential schools, Ottawa, June 11, 2008, https://www.rcaanc-cirnac.gc.ca/eng/1100100015644/1571589171655.

[60] Extract from the full text of Pope Francis's apology delivered in Edmonton, Alberta, July 25, 2022, https://www.cbc.ca/news/canada/edmonton/pope-francis-maskwacis-apology-full-text-1.6531341.

> Colonization is going on rapidly in Manitoba, where legislative and municipal institutions have been established, and where all the characteristics of civilization are fast taking possession of the prairie. In Manitoba there is promise of the same rapidity of development which has been so wonderful in the Western States, for there is the same attraction in the exceeding fertility of soil and bounty of nature. Soon the province will be filled up with a farming population, and the fresh fields beyond must be sought for the purposes of settlement. The government is evidently preparing for this prospective enlargement of our Western empire. Governor Archibald and Commissioner Simpson have just made a treaty at Lake Manitoba with some of the Indians of the western country, which extinguishes the Indian title over a fine tract of well watered country, nearly three times as large as Manitoba. As soon, therefore, as Manitoba fills up, settlers may push beyond her borders and find equal inducements with indefinite expanse of territory. There is an immense future in store for our Great West.[61]

Not everyone shared equally in that future, particularly the Métis and First Nations, who in many cases were pushed off their lands and saw their economies and way of life severely disrupted by colonialism. Many Indigenous people would later experience an even worse fate through the assimilation policies of the federal Indian Act. Thus began a period where the federal government attempted to systematically eradicate First Nations as a people, through efforts to eliminate their culture, language and way of living.

---

[61] *Kingston Daily News*, Sept. 12, 1871.

CHAPTER 9

...

The Fenian Raid

JUST AS LIFE WAS RETURNING to normal for many Manitobans in the fall of 1871, a new threat emerged that could have ended in bloodshed. Instead, it became a unifying moment for the new province—albeit a brief one. It demonstrated that during a crisis, when their community was under threat of attack, Manitobans—Indigenous and non-Indigenous—could put their differences aside and stand together.

Rumours of a Fenian raid from the United States began circulating in September 1871, days after the signing of Treaty 2, raising fears that Manitoba might not be able to protect itself from a military invasion. The volunteer militia from Canada that was part of the Wolseley expedition had been disbanded earlier that year and only a small garrison was stationed at Upper Fort Garry. The threat of hundreds—perhaps thousands—of Fenian Brotherhood soldiers crossing the border into Manitoba sent a chill through the Red River Valley.

The Fenians were Irish Americans who made several failed attempts to invade parts of eastern Canada following the U.S. Civil War. They sought to occupy Canada (or British North America prior to 1867) as leverage in their fight for an independent Ireland. Manitoba, with few regular troops and only a small police force, seemed an easy target. The would-be invaders hoped to persuade disgruntled francophone Métis to join their cause, not only to bolster their ranks but to weaken Manitoba's line of defence.

Irish-born William O'Donoghue—once a key player in Louis Riel's provisional government—was behind the planned attack. In exile for fear of arrest following Manitoba's entry into Canada, O'Donoghue, who had had a falling out with Riel, was hoping to recruit enough Métis to topple whatever forces the Manitoba government could marshal. But to do so, he would need the backing of Riel, who, although himself in hiding for fear of arrest, still had considerable influence over the French Métis.

By October 3 of that year, the threat of an impending invasion was real enough that Lieutenant-Governor Adams Archibald issued a proclamation calling on citizens to form a militia to protect their homeland. There was no confirmation on the size of the Fenian contingent, or even an estimate. Nevertheless, it was considered a serious threat given the large number of Fenians in the U.S., many of whom had fought in the Civil War and had military experience. "We call upon all our said loving subjects, irrespective of race or religion, or of past local differences, to rally round the flag of our common country," Archibald wrote in the proclamation. "The country need feel no alarm. We are quite able to repel these outlaws . . . Rally, then, at once! We rely upon the prompt response of all our people of every origin . . ."[1]

About one thousand Manitobans signed up immediately, and a battalion of two hundred men was sent to the border. The expected invasion turned out to be a bust; the rumours of a large Fenian contingent proved to be false. On October 5, only about forty armed men crossed into Manitoba, some of them Irish Americans. They were arrested almost immediately by U.S. cavalry. The raid wasn't even sanctioned by the Fenian Brotherhood. However, Archibald didn't know that at the time. John O'Neill, who had

[1] Proclamation by Adams Archibald, Oct. 3, 1871, House of Commons sessional papers, 1872, vol. 7, no. 26, 3.

participated in Fenian raids in eastern Canada, was one of the principal organizers. He was captured along with most of the insurgents. The remaining ones scattered, including O'Donoghue, who was captured by several French Métis. He was tied up with rope and handed over to U.S. authorities.

Because fears of a larger invasion still lingered, the lieutenant-governor sought the support of the Métis to help repel a possible second raid. That support was not a given, considering the abuse many Métis continued to endure at the hands of former Canadian militia volunteers and newcomers. The land allotments promised by the federal government had still not materialized more than a year after the Manitoba Act was proclaimed into law. As well, the amnesty promised for those involved in the resistance—including for Riel—remained stalled. Riel was still concerned he could be arrested if he showed himself in public, a fear Archibald attempted to address by getting word to the Métis leader that if he fought for Manitoba, he would not be detained. It was an unusual situation, to say the least, considering Riel was still considered a murderer by many in eastern Canada and could have been prosecuted if apprehended by officials. Despite the risks, and the fact that Riel had been deceived by federal officials more than once since the passage of the Manitoba Act, the Métis leader, remarkably, agreed to use his influence to assemble hundreds of French Métis to protect Manitoba from a feared second raid.

Riel wrote to Archibald confirming the Métis were prepared to protect Manitoba in a letter signed by him, Ambroise Lépine and one Pierre Parenteau:

> May it please your Excellency—We have the honor of informing you that we highly appreciate what Your Excellency has been pleased to communicate to the Reverend Mr. Ritchot, in order that we might be better able to assist the people, in the exceptional position they have been placed in, to answer your appeal. As several trustworthy persons have been requested to inform you, the answer of the Métis has been that of faithful subjects. Several companies have already been organized, and others are in process of formation. Your Excellency may rest

> assured that, without being enthusiastic, we have been devoted. So long as our services continue to be required, you may rely on us.[2]

Archibald was invited to inspect the Métis troops in St. Boniface on October 8 in what became a brief but historic meeting. It is believed he shook hands with Riel during the inspection, a show of conciliation that rankled the anti-Riel crowd, especially in eastern Canada. "I found assembled on the bank 200 able-bodied French Métis; of these 50 were mounted, and a considerable part of the whole body had fire-arms," Archibald later wrote. The Métis cheered and, according to Archibald, told him they had "rallied to the support of the Crown, and were prepared to do their duty as loyal subjects in repelling any raid that might now, or hereafter, be made on the country."[3] Archibald assured the Métis that their show of loyalty would be communicated to the governor general in Ottawa. He later reminded Ottawa that almost none of the French Métis had supported the Fenian "raiders."

"So far as I have been able to learn, there was in the ranks of the raiders one, and one only, French Métis, while the capture of O'Donoghue was made by a number of French half-breeds, who have never swerved in their attachment to the Crown and to British institutions," Archibald wrote to Ottawa.[4]

Over a decade later, Riel said in a newspaper interview that Archibald, during the inspection of the troops, pretended he didn't know who the Métis leader was. "He knew well who I was," said Riel. "I exerted the little influence I had to induce the people all around to oppose the raid. Politically I think that I was the person who in conjunction with the clergy did the most to oppose the Fenian raid."[5]

---

2 Letter dated Oct. 7, 1871, translated and submitted by Adams Archibald to the *Report of the Select Committee on the Causes of the Difficulties in the North-West Territory in 1869–70* (Ottawa: I.B. Taylor, 1874), 147.

3 Letter from Adams Archibald to the People of the Province of Manitoba, October 13, 1871, House of Commons sessional papers, 1872, vol.7, no. 26, 12.

4 Letter from Adams Archibald to Joseph Howe, Oct. 27, 1871, House of Commons sessional papers, 1872, vol. 7, no. 26, 5.

5 *Winnipeg Daily Sun*, June 29, 1883.

Archibald would later face criticism by some officials in Ottawa for his rendezvous with Riel in St. Boniface. Some questioned why he didn't arrest Riel when he had the chance. Warrants had been issued for the arrests of the leaders of the provisional government, including Riel, after the arrival of Wolseley a year earlier. However, the warrants were never acted on by Manitoba officials. In correspondence with Ottawa, Archibald said it would have caused more harm than good to arrest Riel and others. Feelings were still raw between the Métis and Canadian Loyalists, as well as some newcomers. The apprehension and prosecution of Riel and other leaders could have sparked a civil war, said Archibald.

Besides, most legislators in Manitoba believed they had no jurisdiction to prosecute those involved in the resistance, since it had occurred prior to the creation of the province. Manitoba's attorney general in 1872, Joseph Lemay, said during a debate on the issue in the legislative assembly that only the British government had jurisdiction over matters that occurred prior to Manitoba's entry into Canada and that it was up to it to act.

> The native population of this country—who have always acknowledged themselves subjects of England—said we will not become part of the Dominion of Canada till Canada tells us on what terms we enter Confederation. Thus far they were perfectly right. The people arose and barred the entrance of the Canadian government and in doing so paved the way to a great deal of heart-burning and unfriendly feeling. Unfortunately some blood was shed and people cry—why does not the government of Manitoba look after this? Simply because neither the Dominion of Canada nor this province have the slightest right to act.[6]

Archibald also argued it was his duty to bring the French Métis on side to eliminate any potential allegiance with the Fenians. "If I had driven the French half-breeds into the hands of the enemy; if I had shut the door to repentance and prevented them returning to a loyal submission to the

---

[6] Attorney General Joseph Lemay, Manitoba legislative assembly debates, Feb. 5, 1872, in *The Manitoban*, Feb. 12, 1872.

sovereign, O'Donoghue would have been joined by all the population between the Assiniboine and the frontier; Fort Garry would have passed into the hands of an armed mob, and the English settlers to the north of the Assiniboine would have suffered horrors it makes me shudder to contemplate."[7]

The lieutenant-governor claimed he didn't know Riel was among the men assembled in St. Boniface when he inspected the troops. However, he also said he had no regrets if he did shake hands with Riel:

> I shook hands with them all. I did not at the time believe Riel was there . . . But I lay no stress on this. It did not seem to me that it was quite the time, when the country was in danger, to inquire into the antecedents or spurn the offer of any man willing to fight against the Fenians. The whole thing was over in fifteen minutes. On looking back, I see nothing in the course I took that gives me any doubt as to its correctness. I would take it again under the like circumstances.[8]

During his testimony at the Select Committee on the Causes of the Difficulties in the North-West Territory in 1869–70, Archibald said he thoroughly investigated, both before and after the unsuccessful invasion, whether Riel and others were genuinely committed to supporting the government. He said he consulted with independent sources and concluded that the Métis leader and his supporters were sincere in their commitment to protect Manitoba.

Opinions were split in Manitoba over the handshake between Archibald and Riel. Edward Henry George Hay, the MLA for St. Andrews South, said during debate in the legislative assembly that the encounter was inappropriate. "I must say it was an insult to the people when the representative of the Crown went and shook hands with a man who was an outlaw."[9] But

[7] Memorandum by Adams Archibald written between Nov. 5–10, 1871, and submitted to the *Report of the Select Committee*, 142.

[8] Memorandum by Archibald, *Report of the Select Committee*, 142.

[9] Edward Hay, Manitoba legislative assembly debates, in *The Manitoban*, Feb. 5, 1872.

Donald A. Smith, the special commissioner sent by Canada to Red River during the resistance who later won a seat in Manitoba's first legislature, defended Archibald. He said during debate in the legislature that the attacks against Archibald were "totally unfair" and described them as "petty political tricks" waged by critics in eastern Canada.

> I certainly understood that the Lieut.-Governor crossed the Assiniboine and met there a party of French inhabitants of the province, who came armed to protect it in an emergency. I also understood that he shook hands with the leaders of that band without any particular individual having been introduced to him by name. This is my impression and I may say I have had the statement from His Excellency himself... He has been pointed at as a man shaking hands with a rebel, whereas the facts prove that it was with the leader of a body of men coming forward to protect the dignity of the Crown at a most critical moment.[10]

Lord Dufferin, Canada's governor general from 1872 to 1878, also defended Archibald. He wrote several years after the attempted raid, in correspondence to Britain, that the lieutenant-governor's priority was the safety and security of Manitoba:

> Mr. Archibald was alone, cut off by distance from the advice and countenance of the central authorities and thrown entirely upon his own resources. He had no military forces worth speaking of with which to confront the invaders and he was administering a province inhabited by distinct nationalities and distracted by differences of religious faith. Only a few months before, a considerable proportion of its population had been arrayed in arms against the Queen's authority and their fellow subjects. Under these circumstances it can be readily understood that a person in Mr. Archibald's situation would feel it his primary duty to sacrifice every other interest to the defence of the

[10] Manitoba legislative assembly debates, Feb. 2, 1872.

> Province over which he presided, and to the safety of the population for whose welfare he was responsible. Acting upon these considerations Governor Archibald determined to appeal to the loyalty of the French Metis and their leaders.[11]

There were no more attempted raids. Those arrested by U.S. officials were eventually released, including O'Donoghue. Even though the Fenian threat turned out to be of little consequence, Archibald praised those who came together to protect their homeland. "We gave proof to the invaders and to the world that, differ as we might among ourselves on matters of minor moment, our hearts were right and our hands ready when duty called us to the defence of our common country,"[12] he wrote in a summary of his first year in office. However, the loyalty shown by Riel and the Métis was not reciprocated by the federal government. There was still no amnesty and Riel would not receive immunity from the federal government until 1875. That agreement included a five-year banishment for Riel from Canada.[13]

Meanwhile, the distribution of the 1.4 million acres of land promised to Métis families continued to be delayed, newcomers were snapping up some of the most valuable land in the valley, and Riel and Ambroise Lépine, the adjutant general in the provisional government, were forced back into hiding after the threat of the Fenian raid subsided. Even when Riel ran for Parliament (he won three times, in two by-elections and one general election, in the constituency of Provencher between 1873 and 1874), the threat of arrest always hung over his head. He was unable to take his seat in Parliament for fear of being detained, which resulted in the Métis leader being twice expelled from the House of Commons. The closest he came to taking his seat in the chamber occurred on March 30, 1874, when he fa-

---

[11] Letter from Lord Dufferin to the Earl of Carnarvon, Dec. 10, 1875, House of Commons sessional papers, 1875, vol. 7, no. 11, 18.

[12] Adams Archibald, "Manitoba: The History of a Year," reprinted in *Alexander Begg's Red River Journal and Other Papers Relative to the Red River Resistance of 1869–70*, edited by W.L. Morton (Toronto: The Champlain Society, 1956), 420.

[13] The five-year exile the federal government imposed on Riel was from 1875 to 1880.

mously showed up on Parliament Hill, took the oath of office and signed the members' registry. He bolted immediately afterward, concerned about arrest.

Many Métis continued to experience abuse and physical attacks in the streets of Winnipeg following the Fenian raid. Bishop Alexandre-Antonin Taché—who was in frequent contact with Ottawa regarding the persistent mistreatment of the Métis—pointed that out in several blistering letters to federal cabinet minister George-Étienne Cartier. "You do not know all the affronts, privations and even bad treatment we have endured," he wrote in one letter. "Amidst all this, we have kept the profoundest silence, and we have refrained from making known, even to our friends, what was taking place here, in order not to create difficulties for the Ottawa Government."[14]

If the threat of a Fenian raid helped unite Manitoba in 1871, it did little to benefit the long-term interests of the Métis. The loyalty they had shown to Canada during the crisis was soon forgotten. The Fenian raid, and the willingness of the Métis to join forces with the Crown, became little more than a footnote in Manitoba history.

---

[14] Letter from Bishop Alexandre-Antonin Taché to George-Étienne Cartier, May 6, 1871, translated and reprinted in *Report of the Select Committee*, 48.

Conclusion

. . .

WHEN LOUIS RIEL returned to Manitoba to visit family in the summer of 1883, there was little public interest in his homecoming. Riel had steered clear of Manitoba for most of the previous decade; he remained in exile until 1880 mainly because of the execution of Thomas Scott. As time healed old wounds, Riel—who married, had two children and became a teacher in Lewis and Clark County, Montana—was finally free to return home without fear of arrest or persecution.

"Time works wonders," the *Winnipeg Daily Sun* newspaper reported on Riel's return in late June 1883. "Had Louis Riel visited Winnipeg a few years ago, there would have been great excitement and a miniature rebellion. Now there is not a ripple of excitement, and but little interest taken in his presence here. And yet Riel was a most important man in the history of this new country."[1] More than a decade after the resistance, many had either forgotten Riel or never knew of him, "but he will be a prominent figure in history," the newspaper predicted.

By 1883, as Canadians from Ontario and elsewhere migrated to the new

---

[1] *Winnipeg Daily Sun*, June 29, 1883.

province, Manitoba's population had exploded to over sixty thousand people (it reached 250,000 by the turn of the twentieth century). Red River was a much different place from the small community of twelve thousand that Riel had left behind. When two reporters from the *Winnipeg Daily Sun* arranged for an interview and caught up with the Métis leader near the Riel home in St. Vital, he offered a candid account of the resistance.

"I am more and more convinced every day that, without a single exception, I did right," said Riel, fully bearded, wearing a black slouched hat covering his short dark curly hair.[2] "Of course, I don't mean to say my conduct was perfect on all occasions, because every man is liable to make trifling mistakes, but had I the same thing to go through again, I would do exactly the same." That included the decision to execute Thomas Scott. If the people of Canada were aware of all the circumstances surrounding the resistance, they would likely be more understanding of the actions the Métis took, he said. "I have always believed that as I have acted honestly, the time will come when the people of Canada will see and acknowledge it."

By 1883, the number of Métis in Manitoba had declined sharply as a proportion of the overall population. The 1.4 million acres in land grants to Métis families had still not been fully distributed, in large part because of procedural and administrative errors by government and, according to the Supreme Court of Canada, a lack of attentiveness by the federal government to its constitutional obligation. Many Métis families moved west to flee racial discrimination and abuse at the hands of some Canadian settlers. Asked for his assessment on the future status of the Métis in Manitoba, Riel was not optimistic: "There will not be many left in a dozen or so years. They are not civilized enough to compete with the immigrants coming into the country."

It was precisely what Riel and the Métis had feared when Canada announced the purchase of Rupert's Land in 1869. Both the Métis and First Nations faced significant hardship after Manitoba joined Canada, including racial discrimination and persistent attempts by government and the churches to assimilate them into white Christian society. Indigenous people were marginalized and their territory exploited to benefit colonial settlers.

[2] *Winnipeg Daily Sun*, June 29, 1883.

Government did not live up to its obligations under the numbered treaties, including its failure to grant First Nations the amount of land agreed to. Residential schools, and later widespread adoptions of Indigenous children into white families, known as the "Sixties Scoop" in the 1960s, were used by governments in a systematic attempt to eradicate the languages, culture and livelihoods of Indigenous people. Cultural rituals were banned under the federal Indian Act, and many First Nations were prevented from leaving their reserves. Some faced starvation. Indigenous people in Canada were dehumanized through the systematic policies of the federal government.

Those actions violated the most fundamental aspect of the treaties: that Indigenous people would be free to live their lives as they saw fit and would not be forced to assimilate into white Christian culture. The treaties were meant to ensure that neither Indigenous people nor Euro-Canadian settlers would be subservient to the other. That solemn pledge was broken almost immediately after the first of the numbered treaties was signed.

When Canada's prime minister, John A. Macdonald, was asked in 1883 about the effectiveness of residential schools, he confirmed that the institutions existed primarily to assimilate Indigenous children into white culture. He emphasized how important it was to remove Indigenous children from their communities, particularly away from their "savage" parents, to rid them of their Indigenous culture, language and "mode of thought," and the best way to do that was through church-run schools. In a House of Commons debate, he said:

> Secular education is a good thing among white men, but among Indians the first object is to make them better men, and, if possible, good Christian men by applying proper moral restraints, and appealing to the instinct for worship which is to be found in all nations, whether civilized or uncivilized. When the school is on the reserve the child lives with its parents, who are savages; he is surrounded by savages, and though he may learn to read and write his habits and training and mode of thought are Indian. He is simply a savage who can read and write.[3]

---

[3] House of Commons Debates, 5th Parliament, 1st Session, vol. 2, May 9, 1883, 1107–08.

Macdonald appointed himself minister of Indian Affairs to maintain direct control over Indigenous issues. He was a staunch supporter of religious-based residential schools and zealously promoted their use. The prime minster even relished the fact that the buffalo population, which many Indigenous communities relied on for subsistence, was disappearing, because it forced First Nations to abandon their traditional way of living in favour of a "civilized" lifestyle. "It has been strongly pressed on myself, as the head of the department, that the Indian children should be withdrawn as much as possible from the parental influence, and the only way to do that would be to put them in central training industrial schools where they will acquire the habits and modes of thought of white men," said Macdonald.[4]

The prime minister faced regular criticism in Parliament over the increased financial cost of the assimilation process. At least one member of Parliament complained that attempts to assimilate Indigenous people into white society was futile and a waste of taxpayers' money. Philippe Casgrain, a Quebec Liberal MP, told the House of Commons that Indigenous people did not have the aptitude to adopt a "civilized life." He said they would soon become extinct and that further attempts to assimilate them into white culture were pointless. "However good may be the policy of the government and its intentions, they cannot go against the natural law relating to Indians on this continent, and that is, that the Indian race is becoming gradually extinct as the white race advances. That is a broad fact. Another broad fact is, that you have not been able to bring one single Indian to the state of civilization reached by the white man." Casgrain said the "experiment" of trying to assimilate Indigenous people had failed and that it was time to abandon it. "As to the Indians of the North-West Territory, they are a doomed race, and it is only a question of how soon they will disappear."[5]

Casgrain was not alone in his belief that Indigenous people would eventually die off. The Kingston *Daily British Whig* wrote in an editorial that it was important for Canada to make good on its treaty obligations, not so much because it was morally correct to do so, but to protect the country's

---

[4] House of Commons debates, May 9, 1883, 1108.

[5] House of Commons debates, May 9, 1883, 1105.

reputation and to differentiate it from how the United States treated its Indigenous population. "The importance of dealing fairly and in an honorable way with the Indian tribes of the country cannot be over-estimated," the editorial opined. "The unnecessarily severe treatment of the Indians by the Government of the United States and the failure to carry out the provisions of treaties entered into should be a warning to our Government concerning their Indian policy."

The newspaper seemed more concerned about how history would judge Canada in its treatment of Indigenous people than with ensuring the government took steps to support their welfare and to protect their long-term survival. Like Casgrain, the newspaper predicted the ultimate demise of Indigenous people in Canada. "The time will come when the red man will only be known to history for the tribes are fast passing away. Let us hope that the historian of the future will never find it necessary to blame Canada for any cruel treatment or dishonorable dealing with the aborigines of the country, who in times of trouble proved their attachment to, and preference for, British rule on this continent."[6]

History has proved those predictions wrong. Canada's genocidal policies did cause severe intergenerational trauma among First Nations, Métis and Inuit people and shaped the social order that has since prevailed. Despite that, Indigenous people survived, owing in large part to the efforts of Elders and knowledge keepers in preserving their culture, language and oral history over multiple generations. A key part of that survival was reclaiming and preserving treaty and constitutional rights, which successive governments have attempted to roll back since the early days of Confederation. There have been several landmark cases in Manitoba where courts have restored or reaffirmed those rights.

In 2013, the Supreme Court of Canada ruled in favour of the Red River Métis when it found that the federal government had violated its constitutional obligations by failing to properly issue land grants to Métis families:

> The Métis are entitled to a declaration that the federal Crown failed to act with diligence in implementing the land grant provision set out

[6] *Daily British Whig*, Kingston, Ontario, April 2, 1873.

> in s. 31 of the *Manitoba Act*, in accordance with the honour of the Crown. The ultimate purpose of the honour of the Crown is the reconciliation of pre existing Aboriginal societies with the assertion of Canadian sovereignty. Where this is at stake, it requires the Crown to act honourably in its dealings with the Aboriginal peoples in question. This flows from the guarantee of Aboriginal rights in s. 35(1) of the Constitution. The honour of the Crown is engaged by an explicit obligation to an Aboriginal group enshrined in the Constitution. The Constitution is not a mere statute; it is the very document by which the Crown asserted its sovereignty in the face of prior Aboriginal occupation.... So long as the constitutional grievance at issue here remains outstanding, the goals of reconciliation and constitutional harmony remain unachieved.[7]

Over a century after the numbered treaties were signed in Manitoba, more than a million acres of reserve land had still not been distributed to First Nations as legally required under the treaties. The federal government had persistently failed to comply with the terms of those agreements, not only by conveniently ignoring verbal promises made during negotiations, but also by refusing to implement terms agreed to in the written text. Part of that may have been because Parliament, soon after the first numbered treaties were signed, was given false information by Indian Affairs that government had made good on its treaty obligations. As early as 1872, Joseph Howe, the secretary of state for the provinces, which at the time included Indian Affairs, reported, wrongly, that the terms of Treaty 1 had been met. "The stipulations entered into in 1871 have been faithfully fulfilled by the Government in every particular," he wrote.[8]

It took decades of legal action by First Nations to force the federal government to begin the process of fulfilling the terms of the numbered

[7] *Manitoba Métis Federation Inc. v. Canada (Attorney General)*, 2013 SCC 14, [2013] 1 S.C.R. 623.

[8] Indian Affairs annual report for year ending June 30, 1872, House of Commons sessional papers, 1873, vol. 5, no. 23, 3.

treaties. As an alternative to court action, First Nations signed the Manitoba Framework Agreement (MFA) in 1997 with the federal and provincial governments. The MFA established the terms under which individual First Nations could select Crown land, or cash in lieu of land to purchase property, to make up for the land shortfall under the treaties. While the process proved successful for many First Nations (some negotiated separate treaty land entitlement agreements with government), several nations were still forced to resort to court action to exercise their rights under the MFA.

One notable case involved a parcel of land known as the Kapyong Barracks, located in southwest Winnipeg. In 2001, the Department of National Defence announced that the 2nd Battalion, Princess Patricia's Canadian Light Infantry, planned to vacate the 160-acre site on Kenaston Boulevard (coincidently the precise size of land each family of five was promised in Treaty 1) and move to CFB Shilo, located in southwestern Manitoba. The property became surplus federal land, which meant Ottawa had a legal duty to consult with First Nations before disposing of it. The federal government refused, prompting Treaty 1 First Nations to take court action. After an eight-year legal battle, the federal Court of Appeal ruled in favour of First Nations. An agreement was signed in 2019 to transfer two-thirds of the land to Treaty 1 First Nations. Two years later, the Treaty One Development Corporation announced plans to build a mixed-use village on the site featuring commercial, retail and residential properties. Naawi-Oodena (the "centre of the heart and community"[9] in Anishinaabemowin), would be the largest urban reserve in Canada and contribute over $500 million a year to Manitoba's economy.

Naawi-Oodena reflects the vision First Nations had when they negotiated Treaty 1 a century and a half earlier at the Stone Fort: to establish peaceful relations with newcomers and to share the land and its resources equitably. The path to get there in this case—over a century of neglect followed by eight years in court—is symbolic of the struggles First Nations

---

[9] "Naawi-Oodena Officially Converted to Joint Reserve Lands to Become the Largest Urban Reserve in Manitoba," Treaty One website, https://treaty1.ca/t1-joint-reserve-creation-2022/.

continue to face in demanding the Crown live up to its treaty obligations. As a *Winnipeg Free Press* editorial remarked in 2022 about Naawi-Oodena: "Nothing comes easy for First Nations when fighting for their treaty rights—successive federal governments have seen to that."[10]

Manitoba is the only province in Canada whose entry into Confederation was led by Indigenous people. It is a remarkable story of courage and perseverance, but also of racial inequality and social injustice. The broad policy goals of the Manitoba Act and the numbered treaties have yet to be fully realized. They remain a work in progress. However, as First Nations and the Métis build on the visions of their ancestors, and as all Canadians learn more about the relationships pursued in the early days of Confederation and how they apply today, Manitoba and Canada have an immense opportunity to move towards a more equitable and mutually respectful society.

[10] *Winnipeg Free Press*, June 28, 2022.

Epilogue

. . .

LOUIS RIEL WAS LIVING a comfortable life at St. Peter's Mission in Montana in the summer of 1884, almost fourteen years after he was forced to flee Manitoba in the wake of the Red River Resistance. The Métis leader was working as a schoolteacher at the mission, establishing roots in the United States and integrating his family into the local community. Riel, who became an American citizen in 1883, had just moved into a fully furnished cabin on mission grounds, along with his wife Marguerite and two young children—Jean and Marie-Angélique. The man who had challenged the most powerful politicians in the Canadian government and led his people on a daring armed uprising was finally finding peace after years of turmoil, political unrest and threats to his life.

But that newfound solace would be shattered in the summer of 1884. A surprise visit from a small delegation of Métis men from the Saskatchewan District of the North-West Territories on June 4 of that year would change his life forever. Among the four who arrived on horseback was famed Métis leader Gabriel Dumont. They had come to recruit Riel to lead another resistance, this time west of Manitoba. It was an offer Riel, still loyal to the Métis cause, could not turn down. Sadly, it would prove to be a fateful turning point in his life and a tragic end to the fifteen-year struggle for Métis rights on the Canadian prairies.

As settlers poured into the North-West Territories, including the District of Saskatchewan (not yet a province), in the late 1870s and early 1880s, the Métis—many of whom fled Manitoba after experiencing years of hostilities from newcomers—faced the same uncertainties they had struggled with during the Red River Resistance. By 1884 there were still no guarantees Métis land titles would be recognized by the federal government, nor assurances that their way of life would be preserved as Canadian settlement moved westward.

First Nations, for their part, were also struggling to survive on the prairies following the disappearance of the buffalo—their main food source—and remained frustrated with a federal government that refused to honour many of its treaty obligations. Led by Cree Chiefs such as Big Bear and Poundmaker, First Nations were growing restless and increasingly militant as many of their people on the prairies faced starvation. Together with Métis unrest, a political firestorm was brewing on the Canadian prairies.

The North-West Territories were governed by a federally appointed council at the time. When Métis leaders attempted to engage politicians in Ottawa to secure their land and political rights, their efforts fell largely on deaf ears. John A. Macdonald was prime minister again after his electoral defeat in 1873 (he had been re-elected in 1878). Preoccupied with building the Canadian Pacific Railway and settling the west through his "national policy,"[1] Macdonald showed little interest in negotiating with the Métis. Desperate for a new approach, Métis leaders called on Riel for help, hoping he could do for the North-West Territories what he had done for Manitoba: force Ottawa to the negotiating table.

Riel agreed to travel north with his family in the summer of 1884, but he had no intention of remaining in the North-West Territories—at least not at first. He saw himself largely as an advisor, someone who could counsel the Métis on political strategy and help them navigate the complicated world of federal-territorial politics. One of his first tasks was to help de-

---

[1] John A. Macdonald's National Policy was a political and economic strategy that included levying high tariffs on foreign imported goods to protect Canadian manufacturers from American competition.

velop a list of rights similar to the one drafted in Red River fifteen years earlier. Riel had planned initially to return to Montana with his family to resume his teaching duties.

However, the longer he remained in the North-West Territories, the deeper he became involved in the campaign to secure Métis rights. Riel's return to Canada was widely celebrated by the Métis. He was adored by his people. He spoke regularly at packed meeting halls about the importance of building a Métis nation and of the need to protect their collective rights. The support was overwhelming, and it had a profound impact on the thirty-nine-year-old Métis leader. It wasn't long before Riel took on a more defined leadership role.

Riel eventually led a provisional government in the District of Saskatchewan, much as he had done in Manitoba. He attempted to seize control of a Hudson's Bay Company post at Fort Carlton, although he was unsuccessful this time. It burned to the ground before the Métis could take possession of it. Riel also jailed people who opposed the provisional government, as he had done in 1869–70. In some ways, it was the Red River Resistance all over again. However, there were distinct differences.

One of the key contrasts between the two uprisings was that in 1885 the federal government had access to a newly constructed railroad that could quickly transport troops to the prairies to quash any signs of an uprising. Macdonald had not had that luxury fifteen years earlier. Also, the federal government did not have to answer to the British government in 1885 the way it had in 1869–70 when Canada purchased Rupert's Land from the HBC. During the Red River Resistance, the British government had overseen the sale of the territory and urged Canada to use diplomacy with the Métis. It was a political directive Macdonald and his government had not been able to ignore at the time. In 1885, with the North-West Territories firmly under Canada's control, the same political pressure from Britain did not apply.

Armed conflict in the District of Saskatchewan seemed inevitable. The first skirmish broke out in late March 1885 between Riel's men and the North-West Mounted Police, a law enforcement agency created by the federal government in 1873. Unlike the Red River Resistance, blood would spill. After Riel's men began gathering firearms, including ransacking a store in Duck Lake (southwest of Prince Albert), the NWMP were deployed on March 26 to recover the arms and ammunition. Shots were fired, triggering an all-out gun battle that lasted only thirty minutes but resulted in the death of ten NWMP officers and five Métis. It was the first battle in what became known as the North-West Resistance (also known as the North-West Rebellion).

Back east, the federal government began assembling troops to respond to the trouble brewing in the North-West Territories. Some three thousand soldiers, mostly militia members from eastern Canada, were deployed to the region, led by Major General Frederick Middleton. They were joined by another seventeen hundred militia members from the west.

A second battle took place on April 24 at Fish Creek, about twelve miles south of Batoche on the east side of the South Saskatchewan River. Another ten men from both sides of the conflict lost their lives.

Unlike the Red River Resistance, no negotiations took place between the Métis and Ottawa, just gunfights. Some correspondence exchanged hands, but none materialized into anything resembling bilateral talks. Ottawa had no interest in negotiating with the Métis, especially with Riel at the helm. Macdonald regarded Riel as a hostile revolutionary and was determined to capture him and quash the resistance, with deadly force if necessary.

Riel was under no illusion that his small band of armed Métis insurgents could defeat the Canadian military. He hoped that by taking up arms, the federal government would come to the negotiating table as it had in 1869–70. The strategy failed.

The five-month North-West Resistance concluded with a three-day battle in Batoche between May 12 and 15. Métis fighters, numbering only three to four hundred, put up a valiant effort. However, they were no match for the much larger and better equipped Canadian military. Outmanned and outgunned, the Métis eventually ran out of ammunition and were defeated. Riel surrendered to Middleton and Dumont fled to the U.S.

Riel was brought to Regina, where he faced charges of high treason in a trial that was widely criticized for failing to adhere to the judicial standards of the day. The jury was made up of six non-Indigenous English-speaking men, despite the large population of French-speaking Métis in the District of Saskatchewan. Riel's government-appointed lawyers chose insanity as their only line of defense for the Métis leader, even though he opposed it and was later found to be perfectly sane by a government-commissioned psychiatric assessment following the trial. Riel's lawyers refused to make arguments in support of the resistance itself, including why the Métis might have felt it necessary to take up arms to protect their land and cultural rights. Not once did Riel's lawyers take the federal government to task for failing to negotiate with the Métis.

The judge in the case allowed Riel to speak at the conclusion of the trial. In a lengthy address to a small, heavily guarded and packed courthouse, Riel denied assertions that he was insane and made a plea to the jury that the actions of the Métis were justified for the protection of their collective rights. It was an impassioned speech, but it didn't sway the jury, who found Riel guilty on all counts. The Métis leader was convicted and sentenced to hang. After several weeks of delays, including two unsuccessful appeals, Riel was hanged at Regina on November 16, 1885. His body was transported to Winnipeg for burial.

It would be decades before Riel's accomplishments were widely recognized and celebrated in Canada. Manitoba proclaimed Louis Riel Day in 2008, several public institutions have been named after him, and a large statue of the Métis leader stands on the grounds of the Manitoba Legislature. On December 7, 2023, Manitoba's legislative assembly passed legislation making Riel the honorary first premier of Manitoba. To many it was a vindication of the Métis leader's vision and his commitment to the collective rights of all Manitobans, a century and a half in the making.

Selected Bibliography

. . .

Barkwell, Lawrence. *The Reign of Terror Against the Métis of Red River.* Métis Heritage and History Research, Louis Riel Institute. Accessed May 12, 2024. https://www.metismuseum.ca/media/document.php/149078.THE%20REIGN%20OF%20TERROR%20revised.pdf.

Bumsted, J.M. *The Red River Rebellion.* Winnipeg: Watson & Dwyer, 1996.

—. *Louis Riel v. Canada: The Making of a Rebel.* Winnipeg: Great Plains Publications, 2001.

Cheffins, Ronald I., and Patricia A. Johnson. *The Revised Canadian Constitution: Politics as Law.* Toronto: McGraw-Hill Ryerson Limited, 1986.

Craft, Aimée. *Breathing Life into the Stone Fort Treaty: An Anishinabe Understanding of Treaty One.* Vancouver: Purich Publishing, UBC Press, 2013.

Daschuk, James. *Clearing the Plains: Disease, Politics of Starvation, and the Loss of Indigenous Life.* Regina: University of Regina Press, 2019.

Friesen, John W. *The Riel/Real Story: An Interpretive History of the Métis People of Canada.* Nepean, ON: Borealis Press, 1996.

Gibson, Dale. *Law, Life, and Government at Red River, Volume 1.* Toronto: McGill-Queen's University Press, 2015.

Government of Canada. *The Numbered Treaties* (1871–1921). Text transcript of The Numbered Treaties (Treaties 1 to 11). Accessed May 12, 2024. https://www.rcaanc-cirnac.gc.ca/eng/1360948213124/1544620003549.

Howard, Joseph. *Strange Empire: Louis Riel and the Métis People.* Toronto: James Lewis & Samuel, 1974.

Krasowski, Sheldon. *No Surrender: The Land Remains Indigenous.* Regina: University of Regina Press, 2019.

Mailhot, Philippe R. "Ritchot's Resistance: Abbé Noël Joseph Ritchot and the Creation and Transformation of Manitoba." PhD diss., University of Manitoba, 1986. Accessed May 13, 2024. http://hdl.handle.net/1993/3530.

Manitoba Free Press newspaper, September 11, 1919. Accessed May 13, 2024. https://archives.winnipegfreepress.com/.

Manitoba Government. "Origin of the Name of Manitoba." Sport, Culture, Heritage and Tourism. Accessed May 13, 2024. https://www.gov.mb.ca/chc/ourdept/origin_name_manitoba.html.

"Memoir by Louis Riel on the Course and Purpose of the Red River Resistance, Written in 1874." In *Alexander Begg's Red River Journal and Other Papers Relative to the Red River Resistance of 1869–70*, ed. W.L. Morton, 527–49. Toronto: The Champlain Society, 1956.

Miller, J.R. *Compact, Contract, Covenant: Aboriginal Treaty-Making in Canada.* Toronto: University of Toronto Press, 2009.

—. *Shingwauk's Vision: A History of Native Residential Schools.* Toronto: University of Toronto Press, 1996.

Morris, Alexander. *The Treaties of Canada with the Indians of Manitoba and North-West Territories.* Toronto: Willing & Williamson, 1880.

Morton, W.L., ed. *Alexander Begg's Red River Journal and Other Papers Relative to the Red River Resistance of 1869–1870.* Toronto: The Champlain Society, 1956.

—. *Manitoba: The Birth of a Province*, vols. I and II. Altona, MB: Manitoba Record Society Publications, 1965.

New Nation newspaper, January to September 1870. Accessed May 13, 2024. https://digitalcollections.lib.umanitoba.ca/islandora/object/uofm%3A2743729.

Report of the Select Committee on the Causes of the Difficulties in the North-West Territory in 1869–70. Ottawa: I.B. Taylor, 1874.

Riel Papers. In *Alexander Begg's Red River Journal and Other Papers Relative to the Red River Resistance of 1869–1870*, ed. W.L. Morton. Toronto: The Champlain Society, 1956.

Sessional Papers of the Dominion of Canada, 1867–1900. Accessed May 12, 2024. https://www.canadiana.ca/view/oocihm.9_08052.

Siggins, Maggie. *Riel: A Life of Revolution.* Toronto: HarperCollins Publishers, 1994.

Stanley, George F.G. *The Birth of Western Canada: A History of the Riel Rebellions*. Toronto: University of Toronto Press, 1961.

Summit of Treaty Five Sovereign Nations, The. *Treaty 5 Okimaawin Reference Guide*. May 2020. Accessed May 13, 2024. https://www.dropbox.com/s/fwnqzaqfu14ryun/Treaty%205%20Okimaawin%20Reference%20Guide.pdf?e=2&st=ehguohe4&dl=0.

The Manitoban newspaper, 1870 to 1874. Accessed May 12, 2024. https://digitalcollections.lib.umanitoba.ca/islandora/object/uofm%3A2691854.

Wolseley, Garnet Joseph. *The Story of a Soldier's Life*, vol. II. New York: Charles Scribner's Sons, 1903.

Index

. . .

About the Author

. . .

Tom Brodbeck is a journalist who has covered Manitoba and Canadian politics since the mid-1990s. He has written extensively about Indigenous issues, including several features on the Red River Resistance and Treaty No. 1 in the *Winnipeg Free Press*, where he has been a columnist since 2019. Through his writing, Tom was instrumental in helping convince Manitoba MLAs to open their daily proceedings at the Manitoba Legislature with a land acknowledgement. He graduated with a bachelor of arts in economics from the University of Manitoba. When not writing, Tom spends much of his time as a working musician and plays drums for the Winnipeg-based Stephanie Westdal Band.